Daily WRITING & EDITING Practice

BOOK 2

Fabrice Wilmann

First published in 2020, reprinted in 2022

Insight Publications Pty Ltd
3/350 Charman Road
Cheltenham Victoria 3192
Australia

Tel: +61 3 8571 4950
Fax: +61 3 8571 0257
Email: books@insightpublications.com.au

www.insightpublications.com.au

Daily Writing and Editing Practice Book 2 / Fabrice Wilmann

ISBN: 9781922378095 (print)

Cover design, internal design & layout by Gisela Beer
Additional contributions by Laken Ballinger, Melanie Napthine,
Sage Napthine-Morrison & Alison Tealby
Educational consulting by Caitlin Penrose
Editing by Janice Bird
Proofreading by Julia Carlomagno

Printed by Markono Print Media Pte Ltd

Introduction

Daily Writing and Editing Practice Book 2 provides forty weeks of ten-minute daily activities that target the key English skills of writing and editing.

FORTY WEEKLY UNITS

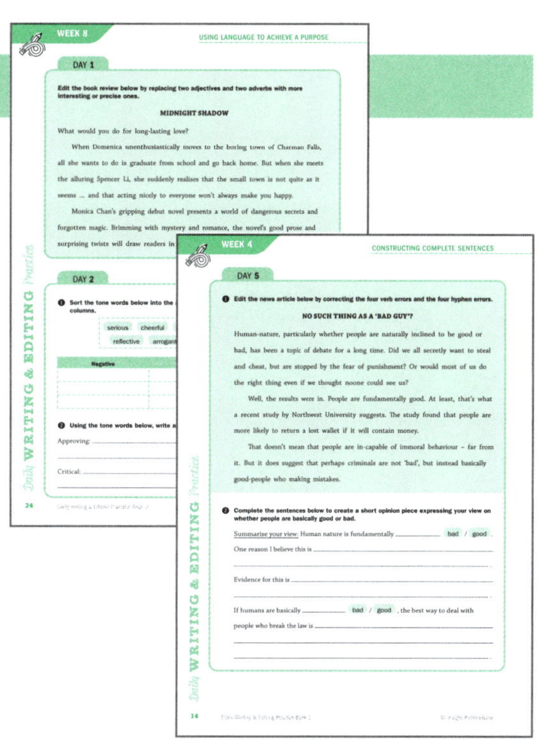

WEEK 8 USING LANGUAGE TO ACHIEVE A PURPOSE

DAY 1

Edit the book review below by replacing two adjectives and two adverbs with more interesting or precise ones.

MIDNIGHT SHADOW

What would you do for long-lasting love?

When Domenica unenthusiastically moves to the boring town of Charman Falls, all she wants to do is graduate from school and go back home. But when she meets the alluring Spencer Li, she suddenly realises that the small town is not quite as it seems … and that acting nicely to everyone won't always make you happy.

Monica Chan's gripping debut novel presents a world of dangerous secrets and forgotten magic. Brimming with mystery and romance, the novel's good prose and surprising twists will draw readers in

DAY 2

Sort the tone words below into the columns.

serious cheerful reflective arrogant

Negative

Using the tone words below, write a

Approving:

Critical:

WEEK 4 CONSTRUCTING COMPLETE SENTENCES

DAY 5

Edit the news article below by correcting the four verb errors and the four hyphen errors.

NO SUCH THING AS A 'BAD GUY'?

Human-nature, particularly whether people are naturally inclined to be good or bad, has been a topic of debate for a long time. Did we all secretly want to steal and cheat, but are stopped by the fear of punishment? Or would most of us do the right thing even if we thought noone could see us?

Well, the results were in. People are fundamentally good. At least, that's what a recent study by Northwest University suggests. The study found that people are more likely to return a lost wallet if it will contain money.

That doesn't mean that people are in-capable of immoral behaviour – far from it. But it does suggest that perhaps criminals are not 'bad', but instead basically good-people who making mistakes.

Complete the sentences below to create a short opinion piece expressing your view on whether people are basically good or bad.

Summarise your view: Human nature is fundamentally .... bad / good

One reason I believe this is ....

Evidence for this is ....

If humans are basically .... bad / good, the best way to deal with people who break the law is ....

Editing tasks

Editing tasks in each week help to consolidate understanding of grammar, punctuation and spelling. Passages for editing are varied and reflect a number of different text types. Examples of how to mark up corrections are included.

Writing tasks

Writing tasks in each week help to consolidate the basic skills of written communication, focusing on expression as well as imaginative, persuasive, informative and analytical writing. The editing passages provide a guide to the forms of writing covered in each week.

ADDITIONAL FEATURES

EXPRESSION 1

Daily checklist

WEEK DAY 1 DAY 2 DAY 3 DAY 4 DAY 5

Vocabulary list

New word	Part of speech (e.g. noun, verb, adjective or adverb)	Definition

Vocabulary list and daily checklists

These sheets can be photocopied and are designed to help monitor progress and keep track of newly acquired words.

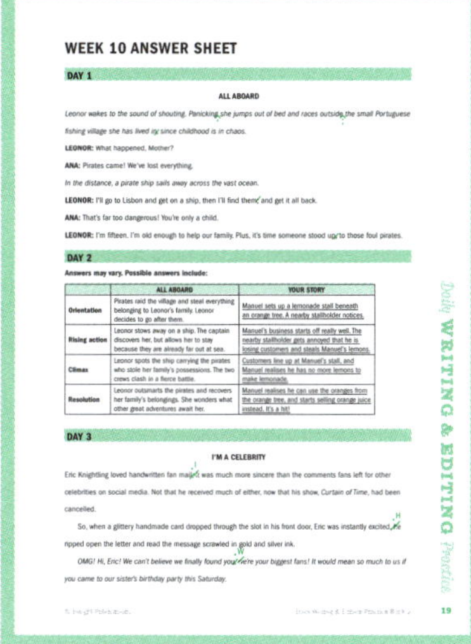

WEEK 10 ANSWER SHEET

DAY 1

ALL ABOARD

DAY 2

Answers may vary. Possible answers include:

DAY 3

I'M A CELEBRITY

Online answer sheets and checklists

Complete answers are provided for each day's activities. For open-ended questions, possible answers are included as a guide. Writing and editing checklists are also available and can be printed for easy access. They identify points to consider when composing and editing a piece of writing. The answer sheets and checklists are available at: **www.insightpublications.com.au/dwep**

Daily WRITING & EDITING Practice

Overview

UNIT 1 EXPRESSION	WEEKS	FOCUS	TEXT TYPE
	1 & 2	Revising parts of speech	Blog
	3 & 4	Constructing complete sentences	Newspaper texts
	5 & 6	Varying sentence types	Advertisement
	7 & 8	Using language to achieve a purpose	Poem/Review

UNIT 2 IMAGINATIVE WRITING	WEEKS	FOCUS	TEXT TYPE
	9 & 10	Plotting an engaging story	Imaginative
	11 & 12	Developing characters and setting	Imaginative
	13 & 14	Using dialogue	Imaginative
	15 & 16	Developing a strong climax	Imaginative

UNIT 3 PERSUASIVE WRITING	WEEKS	FOCUS	TEXT TYPE
	17 & 18	Developing a point of view and contention	Persuasive
	19 & 20	Supporting a point of view with reasons and evidence	Persuasive
	21 & 22	Using persuasive language	Persuasive
	23 & 24	Writing a text to be presented	Persuasive

UNIT 4 INFORMATIVE WRITING	WEEKS	FOCUS	TEXT TYPE
	25 & 26	Brainstorming and researching	Informative
	27 & 28	Organising ideas and creating an outline	Informative
	29 & 30	Using supporting detail	Informative
	31 & 32	Expanding through cause and effect/comparison	Informative

UNIT 5 ANALYTICAL WRITING	WEEKS	FOCUS	TEXT TYPE
	33 & 34	Analysing argument and language	Various
	35 & 36	Analysing argument, language and visuals	Various
	37 & 38	Developing a contention and creating a plan	Analytical
	39 & 40	Using evidence and ending with purpose	Analytical

Vocabulary list

New word	Part of speech (e.g. noun, verb, adjective or adverb)	Definition

Marking-up guide

Use the guide below to help you mark up corrections clearly.

Correction	Example
Make capital letters	rodrigo and charlie are best friends.
Make lowercase letters	Are there Monsters under your Bed?
Add full stops	The play is selling out We should buy tickets now
Add question marks	When is your birthday Is it on Sunday
Add exclamation marks	Help Help My dog ran away.
Add commas	There are lions giraffes monkeys and tigers at the zoo. *
Add semicolons	I did not finish my homework instead, I played tennis.
Add apostrophes	Lets say hello to Sarahs new friend.
Add quotation marks	Welcome to your first English class, she said.
Add hyphens	There is no one more fairminded than my best friend.
Delete text	The parkz is twenty minutes minutes away.
Replace text	Hilda is unliking of spiders and intexts.
Add text	Have ever seen full moon?
Make text italic	Their favourite films are Moana and The Lion King.

* The Oxford comma is not used in this book; the absence of one is not an example of a comma error in the editing exercises. Therefore, there should not be a comma placed before the coordinating conjunction (e.g. and, or) in a list of items.

Daily WRITING & EDITING Practice

EXPRESSION

Daily checklist

WEEK	DAY 1	DAY 2	DAY 3	DAY 4	DAY 5
1	☐	☐	☐	☐	☐
2	☐	☐	☐	☐	☐
3	☐	☐	☐	☐	☐
4	☐	☐	☐	☐	☐
5	☐	☐	☐	☐	☐
6	☐	☐	☐	☐	☐
7	☐	☐	☐	☐	☐
8	☐	☐	☐	☐	☐

DAY 1

Edit the blog post below by correcting the eight spelling errors. The first two have been done for you.

WHY EATING ORGANIC IS THE SMARTER CHOICE

I've always ~~considared~~ *considered* myself a healthy eater who cares about the ~~enviroment~~ *environment*, but it turns out there is a type of food that I've been sorely missing from my diet: organic. What is organic food, you ask? Well, the term 'organic' refers to the way agricultural products are grown and processed. Organic crops must be grown without the use of synthetic pesticides, while organic lifestock raised for meet, eggs and darey products must have access to the outdoors and not be given growth hormones. These proceses, which reduce pollution and soil erosion and increase soil fertileity, mean that organic food is better for the environment. Given that it can be found in most supermarkets, organic food is a no-braner!

Come back next week to read my post on the health benefits of organic food.

DAY 2

Provide three examples for each part of speech indicated in the table below. The first example for each part of speech has been done for you.

! Understanding the purposes of the different parts of speech enables writers to communicate their message clearly to readers.

A **noun** names a person, place or thing.		
lake		
A **pronoun** takes the place of a noun.		
she		
An **adjective** provides more information about a noun.		
curious		
A **verb** identifies an action.		
read		
An **adverb** describes a verb, an adjective or an adverb.		
happily		

Daily WRITING & EDITING Practice

DAY 3

Edit the blog post below by correcting the seven semicolon errors. The first three have been done for you.

THE REAL GAMER

There has been a lot of talk in the online gaming community lately; about 'real gamers' – those who think that the games they play make them superior to others. Real gamers tend to enjoy role-playing games; such as 'CourtFite' these types of games are held in high esteem; because they require many hours of gameplay.

I agree that these games are often more gratifying than simple mobile-platform games however, this is just my personal opinion. It is not fair to suggest that gamers who enjoy a different style of gaming are inferior their tastes are simply different. The scorn directed towards players of the popular farm-themed phone game 'DaisySquash'; is a classic example of this kind of gamer discrimination.

DAY 4

Fill in the gaps with the most appropriate word from the options below for each part of speech indicated. The first one has been done for you.

a **Noun:** A blog (short for 'web log') is an online journal where a writer shares their *views* meanings / views / aspects on a subject.

b **Pronoun:** There are many reasons to start a blog; whatever the reason, ______ that / she / it must appeal to a specific audience.

c **Verb:** Unlike many websites, blogs ______ require / crave / wish frequent updates. For example, a company might update its blog with industry news.

d **Adjective:** Successful blogs are those that have ______ interested / attractive / busy readers who comment on posts and share their opinions.

e **Adverb:** Blog topics are ______ gently / excitingly / mysteriously varied. You can find blogs on an endless number of topics, including food and gaming.

DAY 5

❶ **Edit the blog post below by correcting the four spelling errors and the four semicolon errors. The first two sentences have been done for you.**

HOW TO TRAIN FOR A MARATHON

So, you want to run a marathon? For many ~~runers~~ *runners*, the desire to complete a forty-two-kilometre run is a personal challenge ^; it is a chance for you to test your limits. Whatever your reason, you will need commitment and dedication to achieve this gole.

You should run consistently for at least a year before even contemplating running a marathon it is also a good idea to run a few shorter races in preparation. The key elements of marathon training include the following.

1. **Increase mileage.** Running three to five times per week; allows you to build your weekly mileage over time.
2. **Do regular long runs.** Completing at least one long run every seven to ten days; prepares your body for running long distences.
3. **Recover.** Maintaining normal levels of rest can help prevent injurys.

❷ **Fill in the gaps below to create an idea for your own blog.**

My favourite hobby: ______________________________

This hobby is interesting because ______________________________

______________________________.

My blog will focus on ______________________________.

❸ **Fill in the gaps with an appropriate word for each part of speech indicated to describe your blog.**

a My blog will be very popular because it will include ____________ **(noun)**.

b My blog will ____________ **(verb)** many people.

c My blog can be described as ____________ **(adjective)**.

d People will read the posts on my blog ____________ **(adverb)** because they will be well written.

DAY 1

Edit the blog post below by correcting the seven punctuation errors (semicolons, commas). The first two have been done for you. (Note that the Oxford comma is not used in this book, so no comma is needed after 'boutiques'. See p.vi for further details.)

THE BENEFITS OF OP-SHOPPING

For years I have shopped at highbrow stores, boutiques and fashion outlets; I believed that this set me apart. But, recently, a close friend of mine suggested I go to an op-shop; a charity store that sells new or used goods that have been donated for sale. I discovered that op-shopping is amazing it has both personal and environmental benefits.

Not only is op-shopping a cheaper way to purchase clothes but it is also a fun treasure-hunting expedition. It requires you to rummage through hundreds of unique items to find the one that fits your style finding the perfect scarf or hat can give you a sense of accomplishment. And unlike traditional stores op-shops encourage recycling this helps to keep items out of landfill.

DAY 2

Adjectives and adverbs add precision and detail to sentences.

Fill in the gaps with the parts of speech indicated in the column headings to complete the sentences. Do not repeat any words.

Pronoun	Verb	Adjective	Noun	Adverb
We		delicious		hungrily.
I	jump	tall		
He	builds		tables	
You		big	books	
		shiny	cars	
	are		people	sometimes.
It	sniffs			curiously.

DAY 3

Edit the blog post below by correcting the seven plural errors. The first three have been done for you.

TRICKS TO MASTER PUBLIC SPEAKING

I have given ~~hundred~~ *hundreds* of speeches in my career. There are a few ~~thing~~ *things* that I have learned along the way that will help you achieve ~~successes~~ *success* in any speech you give.

1. **Project confidence.** Public speaking is all about confidence. You don't necessarily need to *be* confident; you just need to make your audience *believe* that you are.
2. **Find a styles that works for you.** Different event often require different approach. While more formal events may call for a prepared speech, others can be more spontaneous and include humour.
3. **Engage your audience.** No matter the type of speech you are giving, you must always make your audience feel as if you are speaking directly to them. Making eye contact is therefore vital to a successful speeches.

DAY 4

Fill in the gaps below with an appropriate word for each part of speech indicated. The first two have been done for you.

A blogger is someone who ___*runs*___ **(verb)** a blog, using it as a ___*platform*___ **(noun)** to share their opinions on ______________ **(adjective)** topics for their target audience. Bloggers can ______________ **(verb)** on lighthearted topics such as food or exercise, or they may choose to tackle more ______________ **(adjective)** subjects such as climate change.

Bloggers who know how to promote themselves ______________ **(adverb)** can earn money with their blogs through a number of avenues. These include ______________ **(verb)** ad space on their blog, marketing digital products such as ______________ **(noun)** and charging membership fees for exclusive content.

DAY 5

❶ **Edit the blog post below by correcting the four punctuation errors (semicolons, commas) and the four plural errors.**

LET'S MEDITATE

Meditation is a mental exercise that involves relaxation focus and awareness. During meditation, which is usually done in a seated position with your eye closed, you think about something very carefully and deeply. There are many scientifically proven benefit of meditation. These include reducing the likelihood of depression reducing stress and relieving headaches.

Learning to meditate is a skill like any other it requires consistent practice. Before beginning, you should try to enter a state of calm by relaxing your bodies and breath. During meditation, it is important to not feel bad about getting distracted it happens to everyone. After each practice, you should aim to write note in your journal.

❷ **Write a short blog post on the topic you outlined in Week 1, Day 5, Question 2. Include at least one example of all of the different parts of speech listed in the table on page 3 in your post.**

Title of blog post: ______________________________

____

____

____

____

____

____

____

____

____

DAY 1

Edit the news article below by correcting the eight capitalisation errors. The first three have been done for you.

MEGA-SHARK TEETH FOUND

Teacher and amateur scientist ~~p~~(P)hilip Mullaly was walking on the beach at Jan Juc in ~~v~~(V)ictoria when he noticed a glint in the ~~S~~(s)and. Looking more closely, he saw a complete set of fossilised giant teeth. Each tooth was seven Centimetres long.

It turned out that the teeth belonged to a rare species of shark that lived in the oceans nearby twenty-five Million years ago.

This rare species of shark grew up to nine metres long, about twice the size of a great white shark. its diet included small Whales.

This set of teeth is one of only three complete sets in the world. mr Mullaly donated the teeth to Museums Victoria.

DAY 2

Place a tick beside the complete sentences below. Place a cross beside the incomplete sentences. Then rewrite the incomplete sentences as complete sentences.

! A complete sentence contains a subject (the person or thing doing the action) and a verb (identifying the action).

- **a** Many fossils have been discovered along the Victorian coast. ☐
- **b** Rare species of shark extinct ☐
- **c** bite more powerful than a Tyrannosaurus rex ☐
- **d** Extreme fear of sharks is called galeophobia. ☐

____

____

____

____

DAY 3

Edit the news article below by correcting the seven verb tense errors. The first two have been done for you.

BRI'S GREAT ESCAPE

Last Saturday, thirty-seven-year-old Bri Sutton ~~will arrive~~ *arrived* at her local beach in the early hours of the morning, intending to ~~went~~ *go* for her usual morning surf. Instead, she finds herself face to face with a shark – and not just any shark, but a great white.

'I'd just coming off my board when I saw it,' Bri recounted. 'My first reaction was to panic, but I somehow will manage to get the board between me and its massive jaws. I guess I was lucky – that seemed enough to scare it off.'

Bri claims that, despite being shaken, she plans to continued surfing at the beach. The shark's whereabouts is unknown, and it could not be reach for comment.

DAY 4

1. **Newspaper headlines often use incomplete sentences to provide the main information in an efficient and attention-grabbing way. Rewrite the headline of the article above as a complete sentence.**

   ____

2. **Create your own headline for the article above, using an incomplete sentence.**

   ____

3. **Modify your headline, turning it into a complete sentence.**

   ____

4. **Fill in the missing parts of speech below to create complete sentences.**

   a Bri ______________ **(verb)** the shark with her ______________ **(noun)**.

   b The ______________ **(adjective)** shark eyed Bri ______________ **(adverb)**.

DAY 5

❶ **Edit the news article below by correcting the four capitalisation errors and the four verb tense errors.**

'JUST MISUNDERSTOOD' SAYS SHARK EXPERT

Renowned conservationist adam Bower will claim that sharks are 'Misunderstood' by many people. He was responding to calls from some members of the public to exterminate sharks to protect beach-goers.

Bower suggests that most species of shark are not naturally aggressive, and that People are less concerned about protecting them due to the way they looking.

'I think a lot of it is because of misinformation,' Bower said. 'If people worked with sharks and knew them like i do, I think they'd see they're not so vicious. Their appearance does them no favours but they were really quite lovely.'

Bower wants people to took the conservation of sharks more seriously.

❷ **Write a short news article on one of the topics below. Use an incomplete sentence for your headline and complete sentences for the rest of the article.**

- Your school report
- A missing packet of biscuits
- An argument with a sibling

DAY 1

Edit the news article below by correcting the seven verb tense errors.

SCARED TO BE LONELY

A recent study has find that people are more afraid of being friendless than of being attacked by a shark or a bear. According to the study, respondents have become so fearful of loneliness that they spending time with people they don't actually like, talk on the phone for hours to fill the silence and left their television on all day so that it seems as though other people will be in the room with them.

Researchers suggesting that fear of loneliness stemmed from people's desire to fill their lives with connections that make them happy. Connection to friends and family is known to be the number-one cause of happiness, and it is important that people take time to focus on nurtured these relationships.

DAY 2

! Including several different parts of speech in a sentence can make it more engaging.

Add the parts of speech specified to the simple sentences below. The first one has been done for you.

a The silver Lamborghini swerved *recklessly* **(adverb)** into the *oncoming* **(adjective)** traffic.

b Greg __________ **(adverb)** hid the glittering __________ **(noun)** in his pocket.

c Mara __________ **(verb)** to the police station to report the __________ **(adjective)** incident.

d Our __________ **(adjective)** Legal Studies teacher explained how innocent people can __________ **(adverb)** end up in jail.

e The judge __________ **(verb)** Karen to 300 hours of __________ **(noun)**.

DAY 3

Edit the letter to the editor below by correcting the nine hyphen errors. The first three have been done for you.

CRIMES AND MISDEMEANOURS

In regard to the study published in your ~~news-paper~~ *newspaper* the other day on morality, I'd like to say that research and statistics are all very well, but real life is not so ~~clearcut~~ *clear-cut*. I have recent experience of ~~ever increasing~~ *ever-increasing* crime rates. Last week, my home-work went missing, presumed stolen. On Saturday, two-thirds of my sandwich just vanished when I turned my back for a second. And yesterday, I found one of my new foot-ball boots had been completely destroyed – vandalised by an un-known attacker.

This 'peer reviewed study' is not much comfort when I am clearly being targeted by some sort of quickthinking criminal mastermind. I can only be thank-ful that at least I have my new puppy, Goliath, to provide me with some protection.

Angry Arnold, Altona

DAY 4

Match the subjects below with the most appropriate verb, then add more information to complete the sentences. The first one has been done for you.

	Subject	Verb
a	Police officers	see ________________ .
b	Criminals	question *suspects and witnesses* .
c	Victims	decide ________________ .
d	Witnesses	are held ________________ .
e	Judges	commit ________________ .
f	Lawyers	suffer ________________ .
g	Prisoners	represent ________________ .

DAY 5

1 Edit the news article below by correcting the four verb tense errors and the four hyphen errors.

NO SUCH THING AS A 'BAD GUY'?

Human-nature, particularly whether people are naturally inclined to be good or bad, has been a topic of debate for a long time. Did we all secretly want to steal and cheat, but are stopped by the fear of punishment? Or would most of us do the right thing even if we thought noone could see us?

Well, the results were in. People are fundamentally good. At least, that's what a recent study by Wynden University suggests. The study found that people are more likely to return a lost wallet if it will contain money.

This doesn't mean that people are in-capable of immoral behaviour – far from it. But it does suggest that perhaps criminals are not 'bad', but instead basically good-people who making poor decisions.

2 Complete the sentences below to create a short opinion piece expressing your view on whether people are basically good or bad.

Summarise your view: Human nature is fundamentally ____________ bad / good.

One reason I believe this is ______________________________

______________________________.

Evidence for this is ______________________________

______________________________.

If humans are basically ____________ bad / good, the best way to deal with people who break the law is ______________________________

____

______________________________.

DAY 1

Edit the advertisement below by correcting the six spelling errors.

HAUNTED HOUSE GENERATOR

Everyone loves a good dinner party – nice music, good food and grate company, all in the comfort of your own home. But as the night drags on, you might start to wander … when are your friends going to leave?

Haunted House Generator is the perfect solution to deal with those guests who just won't take a hint. The Leave-My-House spook pack comes assembled with our best-selling surround-sound system to broadcast the anguished cries of the living dead, along with holograms of vengful ghosts. Need a little more? For the larger home or manshon, upgrade to the Cursed Castle pack, with its selection of grotesque gargoyles and creepy death masks to intimadate your friends and restore peace to your home.

Maintane your social life – on your terms!

DAY 2

Complete the table below with examples of the different types of sentence. An example of each is provided for you.

Effective writing uses a range of sentence types to add variety and emphasis.

A **simple sentence** contains a subject and a verb, and expresses one idea.
e.g. Elaine entered the haunted house.
A **compound sentence** contains two or more linked main clauses, joined by a conjunction.
e.g. Elaine entered the haunted house because she was adventurous.
A **complex sentence** consists of a main clause and a subordinate clause.
e.g. Holding herself steady, Elaine entered the haunted house.

DAY 3

Edit the advertisement below by combining each pair of underlined sentences. The first one has been done for you.

UNISIM

Have you ever wanted to be someone else? Maybe even *something* else? Well, with UniSim by MythTech, you can! ~~MythTech's unicorn simulator uses brain modification technology. It lets you experience the world exactly as you would if you were a unicorn.~~ *Using brain modification technology, MythTech's unicorn simulator lets you experience the world exactly as you would if you were a unicorn.*

The specially designed virtual-reality headset comes fully equipped with mind-altering biopatches. Simply attach the biopatches to your temple. Then adjust the simulation helmet until it's sitting comfortably on your shoulders. Within seconds you will feel like a real unicorn!

* Side effects include dizziness and loss of identity. They also include an increased appetite for hay.

DAY 4

1. **Add extra information to the simple sentences below to turn them into compound sentences. The first one has been done for you.**

   a My brother wants to try UniSim *but he can't afford it* .

   b Adrienne used UniSim yesterday ______________________________ .

   c I'd never thought about being a unicorn ______________________________ .

2. **Fill in the missing gaps to complete the complex sentences below.**

   a Even though ______________________________ ,
   I would be scared of being stuck as a unicorn.

   b While ______________________________ ,
   there are plans to expand the range to other creatures.

DAY 5

❶ **Edit the advertisement below by combining each pair of underlined sentences and correcting the two spelling errors.**

HAPPY HYPNOSIS

Do you ever lie in bed, trying to get some well-erned rest, when suddenly your brain starts powering at full speed? Are you sick of 'zombie-ing' your way through the day? Are you unable to fall asleep at night?

Happy Hypnosis is here to help. An app developed by trained sleep psychologists, Happy Hypnosis contains hundreds of hipnotic recordings. These recordings transform the deeper neural networks of your brain. This will allow you to wake to an inner peace like you've never known before.

Sleep your way to a better tomorrow with Happy Hypnosis.

❷ **Complete the different types of sentences below to create an advertisement for a new product called the Invisibility Cloak.**

Simple sentence: The Invisibility Cloak is ______________________________

____.

Compound sentence: The Invisibility Cloak will be expensive, but ______________

____

____.

Complex sentence: Developed using the secrets of alchemy, the Invisibility Cloak can be used to ______________________________________

____.

DAY 1

Edit the advertisement below by correcting the four run-on sentences. (A run-on sentence consists of two sentences incorrectly joined by a comma.) The first one has been done for you.

ROBOPET

Any pet owner will know that there is nothing quite like the joy of a human–pet relationship. Is there anything better than a cuddle with your pet when you're feeling down?

But do you ever wonder about who's missing out?

We'd like to introduce you to RoboPet, RoboPet makes pets for your pets! It's the all-new robotic answer to staving off pet loneliness, enrich your pet's life by getting them a pet of their own. Are your goldfish bored? Install a RoboFish for them to watch from their tank! Is curiosity killing your cats, buy them hours of entertainment with a RoboCat!

DAY 2

! Using compound and complex sentences allows writers to express more sophisticated ideas.

State whether the sentences below are compound or complex sentences.

a An advertisement is the promotion of a product, brand or service, and its primary purpose is to attract interest, engagement and sales. ________________

b If enough money is invested in advertisements, businesses can reach many users and improve their brand recognition. ________________

c While advertisements are now common in social media and on the internet, they are still widely used in newspapers and on television. ________________

d Advertisements are usually expressed as text but they can also take the form of banners, push notifications or videos. ________________

DAY 3

Edit the advertisement below by correcting the eight punctuation errors (apostrophes, ending punctuation).

TRANSIENT TEE

We at FashionMorph understand the importance of expressing yourself through clothing. We also understand that your interests will change over time and that the effort of keeping your clothing relevant can be wasteful, as well as costly?

Thats why were proud to launch Transient Tee! Got a favourite muscle tee with a humiliatingly outdated logo? Dont want to lose your comfy V-neck, but embarrassed by the TV-show graphic covering the front. Alter your T-shirt design's at whim with Transient Tee, All you need to do is sync our high-quality metamorphic T-shirt with the FashionMorph app. Then you can download whatever image, logo or pattern you like, straight onto the tee! Changed your mind. Clear it and start again!

Reflect your true self with Transient Tee. You'll never buy another T-shirt again!

DAY 4

Add more information to the simple sentences below to turn them into compound or complex sentences. The first one has been done for you.

a Anyone who wears a Transient Tee will become instantly popular.

Regardless of the image, logo or pattern chosen, anyone who wears a Transient Tee will become instantly popular.

b A Transient Tee will save you money in the long run.

____

____

c There are many advantages to owning a Transient Tee.

____

____

DAY 5

❶ **Edit the advertisement below by correcting the two run-on sentences and the two punctuation errors (apostrophes, ending punctuation).**

GALACTIC TRADE

Here at Galactic Trade we offer a variety of undiscovered planets for sale?

Galactic planet's are specifically chosen by our team of astronomical experts to ensure you'll be viewing a range of the highest-quality planets in the universe. There's no need for more endless sifting through barren, rocky planetoids and burnt-out stars, filter your selection through our Galaxy-class search system and let us do the work! From expansive gas giants to lush terrestrial plains, we'll find the planet that best fits you.

Think quality, think Galactic, we can start you on your new journey today.

❷ **Write a short advertisement for one of the products below. Use a mix of sentence types in your piece.**

- A magic carpet that can take you anywhere in the world
- A food printer that produces your favourite food instantly
- Earrings that secretly record conversations

DAY 1

Edit the poem below by correcting the five plural errors.

BREAKFAST

Broken yolk fry slowly in the pan and
Raisin toasts pops up with burned edges and
Empty juice containers sit lonely in the fridge and
All of last night's dish are crusty with food and
Kitchen chair are squeaking across the floor but
Freshly brewed tea is being poured into mugs and
Adventurous lorikeet are flying past the window and
Soft family chatter is filling the room and
Table-talk turns to the possibilities of the day ahead.

DAY 2

Fill in the gaps with the strongest word from the options provided to complete the poem.

! Using precise words can help writers increase the impact of their message on the reader.

Beef ribs have been ______________ smothered / rubbed in dry-rub spices,
Apples have been ______________ well / expertly sliced for the pork-belly dish,
Red cabbage is ready to be tossed in the ______________ tangy / strong dressing,
Basil from the garden has been washed for the tomatoes.
Everyone in the house has been ______________ clamouring / asking for food all day.
Carrying the trays of meat, I call out 'dinner will be ready soon!'
Under the lid, the grill looks perfect and ______________ primed / ready ,
Except that I can't get the charcoal to light.

Daily **WRITING & EDITING** Practice

DAY 3

Edit the poem below by replacing the words in bold with more interesting and precise adjectives. The first two have been done for you.

ICELANDIC SEA MONSTER

The captain so smug as he steered to the sun.
The ~~cold~~ *frigid* air gnawed at my nose.
He told us the number of days – thirty-one –
Since the Hafgufa came out and rose.
My cousin and I were tied fast to the mast,
With ~~thick~~ *harsh* ropes that chafed at our wrists.
We knew that our lives wouldn't last
If we saw the **huge** beast of the mist.

'Get in,' said the captain, showing us the skiff
We'd be using to fight for our lives.
They lowered us down, and we sat tall as if
We'd forgotten that no-one survives.
Our boat moved away from the **scary** ship
A **strong** whirlpool started to spin.
Our hands held on tight with a **hard** grip
As we waited for death to begin.

DAY 4

Fill in the gaps with a word that continues the ABAB rhyme pattern to complete the poem. The first two have been done for you.

Yuichi walked cautiously under the trees
His father not too far behind.
Pink blossoms danced about in the *breeze*
But his future was fresh in his __________
And his heart was churning with *unease*.
Would his father choose to be __________ ?

His father caught up; Yuichi's moment arose:
'There's something that I need to __________ .'
But his father just smiled and dusted his clothes.
'There's a letter you've hidden away,
And I know it's art school you __________ .
But I want you to know it's __________ .'

DAY 5

❶ **Edit the poem below by correcting the three plural errors and replacing the words in bold with more interesting or precise adjectives.**

GLORY

You've always been scared to dance your way into the spotlights,

but today is the day.

Today is the day to ignore those **silly** rule.

Masked faces watch you,

Cool just keeps getting cooler.

But the best gift don't always come wrapped.

It's your turn to discover the world is your runway.

Make a **valid** difference.

Behold the **awesome** magic ... you've had it all along.

❷ **Write a short poem using one of the ideas below or your own.**

- An acrostic poem, in which the first letter of each line spells out a word (see p.21)
- A rhyming poem, in which the last word of every other line rhymes (see p.22)
- A poem expressing an idea or emotion (see above)

DAY 1

Edit the book review below by replacing two adjectives and two adverbs with more interesting or precise ones.

MIDNIGHT SHADOW

What would you do for long-lasting love?

When Domenica unenthusiastically moves to the boring town of Charman Falls, all she wants to do is graduate from school and go back home. But when she meets the alluring Spencer Li, she suddenly realises that the small town is not quite as it seems ... and that acting nicely to everyone won't always make you happy.

Monica Chan's gripping debut novel presents a world of bad secrets and forgotten magic. Brimming with mystery and romance, the novel's good prose and surprising twists will draw readers in and leave them hungry for more.

DAY 2

A writer's choice of words helps to create the tone of a piece. It shows the narrator's attitude or feeling towards a subject.

1. **Sort the tone words below into the appropriate columns.**

serious | cheerful | sarcastic | disgusted | pleased
reflective | arrogant | encouraging | questioning

Negative	Neutral	Positive

2. **Using the tone words below, write a short sentence describing two different books.**

Approving: ____________________

____

Critical: ____________________

____

DAY 3

Edit the theatre review below by correcting the eight capitalisation errors.

BOLD REIMAGINING OF AN OLD CLASSIC

When i first heard that the Lake theatre Company was doing a production of Art Levin's infamous play *rosaline's Sorrow*, I was a little Apprehensive. My fears were eased, however, the moment I heard the first chords.

while the decision to change the original operatic songs into death-metal covers was surprising, I felt it helped to bring the Protagonist's anguish to life, and gave the play a certain modern quality. The Set and costume design were terrific, lending the play an air of authenticity.

My only complaint was that a couple of the Actors appeared to be not entirely familiar with their lines, but it is hard to be critical of such an ambitious work. I could not recommend this play more. Five stars!

DAY 4

Complete the sentences below with interesting adjectives to match the tone indicated.

a **Neutral:** *Rosaline's Sorrow* is a/an ____________________ play that portrays a/an ____________________ take on a traditional love story.

b **Approving:** *Rosaline's Sorrow* is a/an ____________________ play that portrays ____________________ characters who are believable in their various motivations.

c **Condescending:** *Rosaline's Sorrow* is a/an ____________________ play that attempts to be innovative but the story at its heart is ____________________ .

d **Passionate:** *Rosaline's Sorrow* is a/an ____________________ play that everyone must see – a play that will change the lives of people in ____________________ ways.

DAY 5

❶ **Edit the restaurant review below by replacing three adjectives with more interesting or precise ones, and correcting the three capitalisation errors.**

BRAD'S WOK & PIE

situated in the north-west of Cheltenham, Brad's Wok & Pie promises good food at an affordable price, and it was with these hopes that my partner and i went to dine. Alas, the experience was truly terrible. When we arrived the place was in disarray. There was no menu ready for us, the staff were rude, the wait times were really long and, to top it all off, judging by the food, brad seems unfamiliar with both woks and pies. Our big night out was a complete disaster! It's true that, as promised, Brad's is affordable, but the food and service we experienced were a sad disappointment, and I would strongly caution others against going.

★☆☆☆☆

❷ **Write a short review of a restaurant. Remember to use appropriate adjectives and adverbs to achieve your intended tone.**

Intended tone: ______________________________

____

____

____

____

____

____

____

____

____

____

____

IMAGINATIVE WRITING

UNIT 2

Daily checklist

WEEK	DAY 1	DAY 2	DAY 3	DAY 4	DAY 5
9	☐	☐	☐	☐	☐
10	☐	☐	☐	☐	☐
11	☐	☐	☐	☐	☐
12	☐	☐	☐	☐	☐
13	☐	☐	☐	☐	☐
14	☐	☐	☐	☐	☐
15	☐	☐	☐	☐	☐
16	☐	☐	☐	☐	☐

DAY 1

Edit the imaginative piece below by correcting the six punctuation errors (commas, hyphens).

SUMMER

Crystal swung, her old fashioned fishing spear across the front porch and pointed it at Marco. 'Stick 'em up!'

If there was ever a time Marco resented his wild-sister, it was now. They'd come to the beach house early to set up for the annual weekend long family trip – a decision he was quickly coming to regret.

'The fridge is empty,' he said, exasperated. 'The beds aren't made. All you've done since we got here is play with that fishing toy.'

Crystal brandished the spear.

'Hello?' A girl with bright blonde hair, stood at the fence, watching them with a smile. 'I'm Summer your new neighbour.'

DAY 2

An interesting hook (i.e. an intriguing plot detail in the opening scene) can grab readers' attention and make them want to read on.

Describe a possible hook for the following scenarios. The first one has been done for you.

a What if one of your siblings or friends turned into a rat?

While playing hide and seek with my sister, I see a rat. I try to step on it, but stop when I hear my sister's voice coming from the rat.

b What if your teacher turned out to be a robot?

____

____

c What if you were stranded in the bush with your least-favourite person?

____

____

DAY 3

Edit the imaginative piece below by correcting the seven verb tense errors.

FROM THE ASHES

Ioke was shaking. Though she was only halfway up the cliff, the climb has exhausted her. The black rocks feel fragile. She expected to fall at any second.

Ioke had run across the island, following a swift red spot in the sky. Her grandmother had told her stories about magical creatures wandering to their island by mistake, but she had never saw one for herself.

'Ouch!' Ioke will say as her leg scraped the rough volcanic stones. She mistakenly looks down, and her stomach dropped, but her curiosity drove her on, and she keeps reaching for the top. With great effort, she pulled herself up over the edge, and finally finds the red creature: a beautiful, vibrant phoenix, waiting to die in its nest.

DAY 4

Turn the everyday situations below into interesting story ideas by asking a 'What if' question. The first one has been done for you.

a Leilani finds a key to the locked attic door.

What if *Leilani discovered that her attic is home to a secret community of fairies*?

b Manuel sets up a lemonade stand.

What if ____?

c There is a school fair, attended by the principal.

What if ____?

d Paulo asks Lydie to the school dance.

What if ____?

DAY 5

❶ **Edit the imaginative piece below by correcting the four punctuation errors (commas, hyphens) and the four verb tense errors.**

AWAKENING

The sun was beating down hard. Mary sits cross-legged in her backyard, surrounded by weeds so overgrown that they could double as Amazonian tree ferns. Mary's mother had told her daughter that she will receive no more allowance until she pulled out all of the weeds, which Mary found quite unfair. It would take her several week-ends to clear out all these weeds.

Mary crawled through the jungle of weeds, pulls them out one at a time. After a few minutes of hard work (and angry mumbling), she had to take a break. It was in this moment, among the bric-a-brac of potted plants and garden gnomes that she discovered a golden lamp.

She picked it up and rubbed it gently. A whirring noise, filled the backyard as a giant-golden genie erupting from the lamp.

❷ **Using one of the 'What if' questions from Day 4, or your own 'What if' question, write an engaging opening scene to an imaginative piece.**

DAY 1

Edit the imaginative piece below by correcting the five punctuation errors (semicolons, commas).

ALL ABOARD

Leonor wakes to the sound of shouting. Panicking she jumps out of bed and races outside the small Portuguese fishing village she has lived in, since childhood is in chaos.

LEONOR: What happened, Mother?

ANA: Pirates came! We've lost everything.

In the distance, a pirate ship sails away across the vast ocean.

LEONOR: I'll go to Lisbon and get on a ship, then I'll find them; and get it all back.

ANA: That's far too dangerous! You're only a child.

LEONOR: I'm fifteen. I'm old enough to help our family. Plus, it's time someone stood up, to those foul pirates.

DAY 2

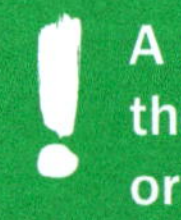

A plot generally includes the following elements: orientation, rising action, climax and resolution.

Using the example below as a guide, complete the table for your own story idea. (You can use one of the 'What if' questions from Week 9, Day 4 or an original idea.)

	ALL ABOARD	YOUR STORY
Orientation	Pirates raid the village and steal everything belonging to Leonor's family. Leonor decides to go after them.	
Rising action	Leonor stows away on a ship. The captain discovers her but allows her to stay because they are already far out at sea.	
Climax	Leonor spots the ship carrying the pirates who stole her family's possessions. The two crews clash in a fierce battle.	
Resolution	Leonor outsmarts the pirates and recovers her family's belongings. She wonders what other great adventures await her.	

DAY 3

Edit the imaginative piece below by correcting the three run-on sentences.

I'M A CELEBRITY

Eric Knightling loved handwritten fan mail, it was much more sincere than the comments fans left for other celebrities on social media. Not that he received much of either, now that his show, *Curtain of Time*, had been cancelled.

So, when a glittery handmade card dropped through the slot in his front door, Eric was instantly excited, he ripped open the letter and read the message scrawled in gold and silver ink.

OMG! Hi, Eric! We can't believe we finally found you, we're your biggest fans! It would mean so much to us if you came to our sister's birthday party this Saturday.

Yours truly, Kay and Mia.

'Well,' he said to himself, 'it sounds like I'm going to a party.'

DAY 4

Describe possible rising action for the scenarios below. The first one has been done for you.

SCENARIO	RISING ACTION
Leilani discovers a secret community of fairies in her attic.	*The fairies are evil and try to banish Leilani to a different dimension where there are no mobile phones or social media.*
Manuel and his friend Igor have a competition to see who can earn the most money from selling lemonade.	
Principal McPhee attends the school fair and announces that all students must perform a song for the audience.	
Paulo asks Lydie to the school dance but she has already said yes to someone else.	

DAY 5

❶ **Edit the imaginative piece below by correcting the two punctuation errors (semicolons, commas) and the two run-on sentences.**

THE GREAT WALL

Li Jun grunted; as he lifted the oat-coloured bricks from the cart to the foot of the wall. He dropped the bricks with a thud onto the soft earth and stood back, admiring his handiwork. The project was really coming together, he was sure it would be a great wall one day.

As he placed the new bricks onto the growing wall, he could hear his fellow workers gossiping quietly under their breath, their voices carried by the wind, Li didn't like distractions; he was totally committed to the task Emperor Yong had assigned him.

Li Jun was so focused on his work, that he did not hear the barbarian sneak up behind him.

❷ **Write a short scene of rising action based on your story outline from Day 2.**

___

___

___

___

___

___

___

___

___

___

___

DAY 1

Edit the imaginative piece below by correcting the six spelling errors. The previous part of this story is on page 29.

SUMMER

After Summer left, Marco went to buy the grocerys. Crystal had gone off with her fishing spear, clearly not interested in helping.

It didn't take long too reach the trail leading to town. Away from the main road, Marco could see brite blue flashes of ocean between the thin trees lining the trail. The site of the ocean always made him feel at ease. Sometimes things at home could get so crazy, especially with Crystal being the way she was. But the ocean reminded Marco of days at the beach with his friends, or swiming by himself in the calmness of the gentel waves.

'Marco?' Summer stood unobtrusively by one of the trees, hair dripping as though she'd just come out of the water.

DAY 2

Writers need to know their characters thoroughly in order to bring them to life on the page.

Fill in the boxes below to form a description of a main character.

NAME:

AGE: **HOME TOWN:**

PERSONALITY TRAITS (e.g. proud, sarcastic, caring):

GREATEST ACCOMPLISHMENTS:

DREAMS & FEARS:

DAY 3

Edit the imaginative piece below by correcting the five subject–verb agreement errors. The first two have been done for you. **The previous part of this story is on page 30.**

FROM THE ASHES

The smell of fish ~~were~~ *was* wafting down the dirt road as Ioke made her way home. Two dogs ran by her, and she could hear a rooster ~~crows~~ *crow* nearby. Ioke looked down at her hands and knees. They was bleeding slightly from her climb. Someone would notice as soon as she walked in the door, and then the whole family would be asking questions, demanding answers. The tears of a phoenix has healing powers, but would anyone believe her?

Ioke walked slowly up the front steps to her house. Through the open window, she could hear the clattering of pans in the kitchen, and her brother were arguing with their mother. Maybe keeping the phoenix a secret was best for everyone.

DAY 4

Describe how the main character you developed in Day 2 would respond to the following scenarios.

a Their best friend or close family member goes missing. ______________________

____

____

b They are asked to give a speech at a school assembly. ______________________

____

____

c They discover an abandoned mansion in the middle of the bush. ______________________

____

____

DAY **5**

❶ **Edit the imaginative piece below by correcting the four spelling errors and the four subject–verb agreement errors.** **The previous part of this story is on page 31.**

AWAKENING

Mary couldn't believe her eyes. A real-life genie were floating before her. His body was transluscent, and he had silver-grey hair that sat atop his head like a glittary mop.

'What are you?' Mary stuttered.

'Why, I are a genie, of course,' replied the genie. 'I thought the lamp made that rather obvious. Anyway, I is here to grant you any wish you desire.'

'I does not need a genie or any wishes, thank you. My life is perfect as it is.'

'No-one's life is perfect,' the genie said noingly. 'Be honest with me.'

Mary thought for a wile. There was only one thing that she truly wanted. Something she had wanted her whole life, but never had: a best friend.

❷ **Using one of the scenarios from Day 4, write a short scene that develops your main character.**

____

____

____

____

____

____

____

____

____

____

DAY 1

Edit the imaginative piece below by correcting the six spelling errors. The previous part of this story is on page 32.

ALL ABOARD

Leonor breathes in the salty air as she soaks in the vibrent, bustling atmostphere of one of Portugal's great cities.

LEONOR: I can't believe it! I've dreamed for so long of travelling to Lisbon, and now I'm finally here.

Determination etched on her face, Leonor makes her way to the port, which is full of ships.

LEONOR: I need to find a ship to help me track down those pirates. But it won't be eazy. Succesful sea captains don't usually let strange kids aboard.

Leonor looks out to the sea, which sparkles like a jewl. She spots the opportunity she's been looking for: a ship whose crew is knowhere in sight.

DAY 2

Using descriptive language, describe a potential setting for the story ideas below. The first one has been done for you.

Writers describe the location or environment of a story in great detail so that the reader can better picture the scene.

STORY IDEA	POTENTIAL SETTING
Paula plans to steal jewels from the royal family of Spain and sell them to the highest bidder.	*The ivory castle was spellbinding, its spires glimmering like shards of crystal in the moonlight. The rooms inside were equally mesmerising, but none more so than the jewel room, which glittered like the stars in the sky above.*
Sergio goes snorkelling at the Great Barrier Reef, trying to discover a new species of coral.	
Imelda rushes her brother to the hospital after he falls off his bicycle.	
Khanh is offered an internship at the most famous restaurant in Beijing and must prove his worth to the other chefs.	

DAY 3

Edit the imaginative piece below by replacing the words in bold with more interesting or precise adjectives. The previous part of this story is on page 33.

I'M A CELEBRITY

Eric spent three hours selecting a **good** outfit. He finally settled on his second-best blue blazer and the most expensive pair of **nice** jeans that he owned.

When he reached the address on the invitation, he expected to see a **big** mansion. Or really, any type of mansion. Instead, he was on the lawn of a very **normal** house. There was a **hard** driveway and a faded yellow door, and Eric swore he could hear cows mooing in the distance.

Someone inside the **dull** house screamed, and suddenly a swarm of **loud** teenagers was coming through the yellow door. Eric struck his best pose, but when he looked at the crowd, no-one was smiling.

DAY 4

Create a plot for each of the settings below. The first one has been done for you.

SETTING	PLOT
A fancy boarding school in another country	*A young girl from rural Queensland is accepted into a prestigious boarding school in Cambridge, England. All the other students there mock her because she has a strange accent. She wins them over by playing the didgeridoo at the school talent show.*
A shopping centre after closing hours	
A family home in the countryside	
A marketplace on an alien planet	

DAY 5

❶ **Edit the imaginative piece below by correcting the three spelling errors and replacing the words in bold with more interesting or precise adjectives.** **The previous part of this story is on page 34.**

THE GREAT WALL

The barbarian wrestled Li Jun to the ground. Li struggled, flaling his arms wildly in an attempt to disrupt his kaptor. But it was futile.

Then he remembered something his **brainy** father had once told him: *there is much power in stillness*. He stayed completely still. The barbarian thought he had won the battel and loosened his grip. It was in that moment that Li pounced. He pushed his head back, throwing the **spooked** barbarian off him.

Li stood up and looked at the barbarian. 'You may have slain my father, but I won't let you barbarians harm any more of my people.'

With that **scary** warning ringing in his ears, the barbarian fled.

❷ **Write a short scene in which a character from one story appears in the setting of another (e.g. Spiderman at Hogwarts School of Witchcraft and Wizardry).**

Character from one story: ______________________________

Setting from another story: ______________________________

____

____

____

____

____

____

____

____

____

DAY 1

Edit the imaginative piece below by correcting the seven quotation mark errors. The first two have been done for you. **The previous part of this story is on page 35.**

SUMMER

‘ Hey, Summer.’ Marco walked over to her, feeling awkward.

‘The water is so lovely,’ ’ Summer said. Come for a swim?’

‘Heading into town. I should …’ He hesitated. The water really did look inviting in the day’s heat. ‘Maybe a quick one, just to cool off.

‘She beamed, then rushed down towards the beach. Marco trailed behind. By the time he reached the sand, only her head was visible above the water.’

Marco kicked off his shoes and waded knee-deep into the ocean, sighing at the touch of the cool waves. Summer?’

She turned back and smiled, revealing a long row of sharply pointed teeth.

DAY 2

State which line of dialogue best reflects each character and explain your choice.

> **!** Good dialogue is believable and reflects the personality of the character who is speaking. It should advance the plot and reveal the thoughts and feelings of the characters.

a ‘Geez Louise, it’s rather nippy,’ said Marco.

‘Yikes, the water’s so cold,’ said Marco.

____

____

b ‘You’re a really good swimmer,’ said Summer.

‘Your breaststroke technique is quite impeccable,’ said Summer.

____

____

Daily **WRITING & EDITING** Practice

DAY 3

Edit the imaginative piece below by correcting the seven verb tense errors. **The previous part of this story is on page 36.**

FROM THE ASHES

'I thought I might find you out here.'

Ioke will look up from feeding the chickens. Her grandmother was hobbling out of the house towards her. 'You are quiet during dinner,' she said.

Ioke nodded, throwing a handful of corn. 'Just tired, that's all.'

Her grandmother comes closer before pulling a red feather out of her pocket. Ioke's eyes will widen.

'This falls out of your hair when you came in,' she says cheekily. 'They say that tears of a phoenix can heal anything, even your brother's blindness.'

'But Kaleo would never believe me,' said Ioke.

'Ioke, you'll never know unless you asked him.'

DAY 4

Rewrite the scenario below as dialogue between Ioke and Kaleo.

Ioke approached Kaleo and told him she wanted to take him somewhere the following morning. Kaleo was curious, asking many questions. Ioke replied that he didn't need to know the answers; he just needed to trust his big sister. Kaleo finally accepted what his sister was saying, agreeing to go without further discussion.

Ioke: ______________________________

Kaleo: ______________________________

Ioke: ______________________________

Kaleo: ______________________________

Ioke: ______________________________

Kaleo: ______________________________

DAY 5

❶ **Edit the imaginative piece below by correcting the four quotation mark errors and the four verb tense errors.** The previous part of this story is on page 37.

AWAKENING

Before Mary could stop herself, the words spurted out: 'I wish for a best friend.'

'Your wish was my command, the genie said with a wicked grin.

The ground jolted. Mary's breath grew shallow. *What's happening*? she thought. *Did I just make a terrible mistake?*

'BOY,' said a rasping voice from behind Mary, 'I sure do not expect THAT!'

Mary looked around. 'A squat concrete gnome was standing at her feet. It had thick white eyebrows set over the heavy features of an old-man scowl.'

'Hi, missy,' the gnome snarled. 'I'm your new best friend!'

Mary slumped to the ground, dropping the lamp beside her. This is not what she had in mind when she had wished for a best friend. She looked at the genie, who will be laughing maniacally.

❷ **Fill in the blank lines below to complete the play script.**

A: I'm sorry, Gerald. I have no choice but to trap you in the form of a gnome, destined to spend the rest of your days as a lawn ornament.

B: Please, Jasper, you can't! Why are you doing this to me? I thought we were friends. Ever since you became a genie, you've changed.

A: ______________________________

____

B: ______________________________

____

A: ______________________________

B: ______________________________

DAY 1

Edit the imaginative piece below by correcting the six subject–verb agreement errors.
The previous part of this story is on page 38.

ALL ABOARD

Leonor hides aboard a ship about to set sail. The captain discover her and is furious.

CAPTAIN: Oi! What are you doing here?

LEONOR: I is here to find the pirates who attacked my village and stole my family's possessions. Please let me stay onboard!

The captain sees how desperate Leonor is and smile grudgingly.

CAPTAIN: Okay, you can stay. But only because we're already so far from shore. Just don't get in the way of my crew.

The next day, Leonor spots a familiar ship in the distance.

LEONOR: Captain, I thinks those are the pirates who attacked my village!

CAPTAIN: I knows them. They causes absolute havoc on these seas. Let's put an end to their terror once and for all!

DAY 2

Fill in the gaps in the story below with dialogue.

Dialogue helps to break up long passages of description, and vice versa.

Leonor sat in silence as she watched Gregorio and Julio hoist the sails. These two burly men were the hardest-working crew members on the ship, and Leonor admired them greatly.

'____?' asked Leonor.

'The captain taught us,' replied Julio. '____

____. So you can see why it's not so easy to learn!'

The other crew members scrambled about the ship, preparing to engage in battle with the pirates on the approaching vessel.

'Are you scared, little Leonor?' asked Gregorio as he climbed down the mast.

'______________________________,' said Leonor. '______________________________

____.'

DAY 3

Edit the imaginative piece below by correcting the seven punctuation errors (apostrophes, hyphens). **The previous part of this story is on page 39.**

I'M A CELEBRITY

A girl in a yellow party dress stepped forward, studying Eric carefully.

'Who are you?'

'Im Eric Knightling,' he said confidently. 'And you are?'

'Oh no!' she said, turning to her sister. 'Mia, we sent the card to the wrong Eric!'

A girl in a sparkly green dress pushed through the crowd, shiny-tears in her eyes. 'You mean Eric Kinesy isnt coming?'

'Eric Kinesy?' he asked, standing embarrassed on the lawn. 'You were trying to invite that well known actor from the weird yeti show?'

The girl in yellow came closer so that the others wouldnt hear. 'I'm really sorry, Mr Knightling, for making you come all this way. It was an honest-mistake. But youre welcome to stay for the party if you want.'

DAY 4

Fill in the gaps in the story below with description.

____.

'What about hide and seek or pass the parcel?' suggested Mia. 'Or duck, duck, goose could be fun, maybe ...'

____

____.

'What are we going to do?' Mia whispered to Kay. 'This party is turning into a disaster!'

____

____.

'Let's try that. At this point, what do we have to lose?' Mia said.

Daily WRITING & EDITING Practice

DAY 5

❶ **Edit the imaginative piece below by correcting the three subject–verb agreement errors and the three punctuation errors (apostrophes, hyphens).** **The previous part of this story is on page 40.**

THE GREAT WALL

Li could hears applause all around him. Everyone who had seen the skirmish were now checking to see if he was okay – not only his fellow workers, but also the general, Wang Wei.

'Well done, Li,' said Wang. The generals pheasant-tail headdress, which he wore to distinguish himself from the peasants, rustled softly in the breeze.

'Thank you, General. I simply followed one of my father's-favourite proverbs,' Li replied shyly, fumbling with the cord of his pants.

'Youve served your emperor well,' said Wang. 'You will be rewarded for your loyalty and bravery. I will brings you to meet Emperor Yong.'

❷ **Using dialogue and description, write a short scene between the main character you developed in Week 11 (pp.35–7) and a secondary character.**

DAY 1

Edit the imaginative piece below by correcting the seven verb tense errors. **The previous part of this story is on page 41.**

SUMMER

Marco stumbled back, seeing Summer's pupils expand until they were deep pools of darkness.

She rushes at him, cutting through the water like a torpedo. Marco turned to swam away, but Summer was much too fast.

Crystal stands at the edge of the water, her spear poised.

'Hey, Fish Face, take that!'

The water will explode in an enormous splash. Summer let out a furious growl and lunging forward. But Crystal grabbed Marco's flailing arms, hauling him out of the water.

'Seems like it was a good day to practising spearfishing after all,' Crystal said.

Marco and Crystal ran away, left an infuriated Summer alone in the water.

DAY 2

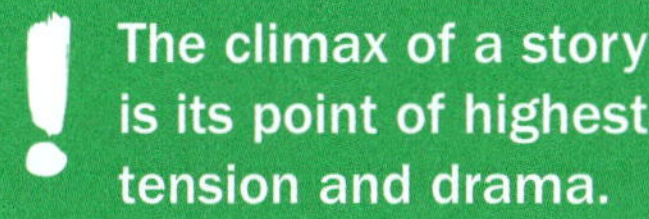

! The climax of a story is its point of highest tension and drama.

1 **In your own words, describe the climax in the story above.**

____

____

2 **State which of the following events you think is a more interesting alternative climax for the story above and explain your choice.**

a Summer has sharp teeth because she only eats soft food. Marco's horrified reaction makes her feel ugly and she runs away in tears.

b Summer's pupils expand because she is an alien who has come to take Marco away to her home planet.

____

____

DAY 3

Edit the imaginative piece below by correcting the five spelling errors. **The previous part of this story is on page 42.**

FROM THE ASHES

The wind was a howling wolf, whipping at Ioke and Kaleo as they sat atop the cliff. The green island stretched out beneaf them, a butiful image of their home.

'I can't beleave we made it,' Kaleo said. 'Being up this high is incredable.' They were sitting on soft grass, where a pile of ash smouldered in the middle of a nest.

Ioke stared harder into the nest and saw a small red bird raise its head from the ashes. The young phoenix sang to them, as sweet as the sunrise, and tears began falling from its face. Ioke held out her hand and felt the tears on her fingertips. She then placed them onto her brother's eyelids.

Kaleo turned to look at Ioke. And he really looked at her, his eyes full of unbridled delite. A river of tears flowed down his cheeks.

DAY 4

Describe a possible climax for the scenarios of rising action below. The first one has been done for you.

RISING ACTION	CLIMAX
Ioke and Kaleo climb a treacherous cliff to find the mythical phoenix.	*They find the bird and use its tears to heal Kaleo's blindness.*
Leilani discovers evil fairies who try to banish her to a different dimension where there are no mobile phones or social media.	
Manuel and his friend Igor begin playing dirty tricks on each other in order to sell more lemonade and win the competition.	
Lydie regrets agreeing to go to the school dance with Lebron because she really wants to go with Paulo. She contemplates what she should do.	

DAY 5

❶ **Edit the imaginative piece below by correcting the four verb tense errors and the four spelling errors.** **The previous part of this story is on page 43.**

AWAKENING

Mary survaid the mess before her. There was a gnome running around her backyard like a wild coyote, and a mischeivous genie floating about cackling to himself like an evil witch. Mary had to clear up this mess quickly, but how?

Of course! Why hadn't she thought about that before? Genies always granted three wishes. That meant she have another two wishes left!

'Mr Genie,' she yelled confidently, 'I wish to undo my first wish.'

The genie stopped laughing immediately and crossed his arms angryly. He had no choice but to grant Mary her wish. Just like that, the gnome drops like a stone.

'And for my last wish I want you to get rid of all these weeds!'

Again, the genie did as he was instructed. And with that final wish, he vanishes back into the lamp. Mary bent down in releaf. She will have done it.

❷ **Write a climactic scene based on the rising action scene you wrote in Week 10, Day 5, Question 2 (p.34).**

DAY 1

Edit the imaginative piece below by combining each pair of underlined sentences. The first one has been done for you. The previous part of this story is on page 44.

ALL ABOARD

The captain and his crew board the pirate ship, followed by Leonor. Swords dip like gulls as the two crews clash.

Leonor's heart hammers as she valiantly fights on.

~~*Leonor's heart hammers. She valiantly fights on.*~~

LEONOR: How are we going to defeat all these pirates?

Suddenly, the answer appears. It is like a lighthouse on a stormy night. Leonor steers the fight towards the edge of the ship. She keeps her balance. The clumsier pirates slip overboard.

CAPTAIN: Leonor, you've saved the day!

After the battle, Leonor gazes out across the sea, spread out before her like a dark blanket.

LEONOR: I can't go home now. I am longing for new adventures.

DAY 2

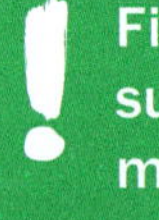

Figures of speech, such as similes and metaphors, draw unexpected comparisons to create vivid images.

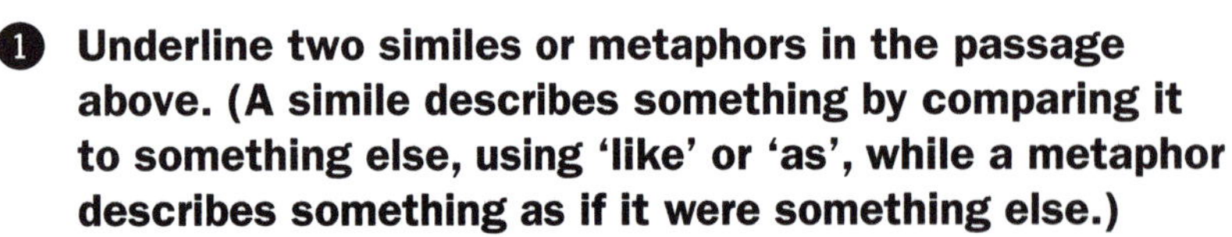

1. **Underline two similes or metaphors in the passage above. (A simile describes something by comparing it to something else, using 'like' or 'as', while a metaphor describes something as if it were something else.)**

2. **State which figure of speech you find more engaging, and explain your choice.**

   a She hung her head like a dying flower.

   Her hair was as soft as a cuddly toy.

   ____

   b I appreciate you like a gorilla appreciates a grammar book.

   The classroom was as quiet as a deserted lolly shop.

   ____

DAY 3

Edit the imaginative piece below by replacing the words in bold with more interesting or precise adjectives. **The previous part of this story is on page 45.**

I'M A CELEBRITY

Eric hesitated before bravely walking into the house. The party guests were sprawled out over the living room like **still** slugs. The **big** birthday cake hadn't been touched, and Kay and Mia were trying to console their **sad** sister. Eric looked around for inspiration, and he noticed a box set of *Curtain of Time* on the shelf.

'Pardon me,' he said, startling the room. 'But have any of you actually seen my show?' The guests all shook their heads. Eric knew exactly what to do.

Seven episodes and three slices of **yummy** cake later, the party guests and the sisters were gathered around Eric, cheering when he quoted his lines perfectly and gasping at the **strong** dramatic scenes.

'This is amazing!' said Kay. 'I guess we did invite the right Eric after all!'

DAY 4

1. **Create your own figures of speech by filling in the gaps with an imaginative comparison.**

   a As tall as ______________________________.

   b As clever as ______________________________.

2. **Figurative language should be used sparingly. Delete three figurative phrases from the passage below to create a more compelling piece of writing.**

   Max pulled his coat tightly around himself. Ice mountains surrounded him from every direction, their peaks jagged like broken glass. The cold was as icy as a freezer and so fierce even the slightest breeze felt sharp as a knife.

   It had been three months since he'd begun searching for the mythical yeti, but it felt like years. Three months of camping like a hermit in the frozen valley. Most days, mist would rise from the snow, dense as a cloud and white as cotton. But today the air was crystal clear, fragrant as springtime and full of potential.

DAY 5

❶ **Edit the imaginative piece below by combining each pair of underlined sentences and replacing the words in bold with more interesting or precise adjectives.** **The previous part of this story is on page 46.**

THE GREAT WALL

Li breathed in sharply. He could hardly believe it. He was in the Forbidden City. He was staring at the emperor of China. Emperor Yong was as **glossy** as the sun, with hair as dark as the night sky. Li bowed graciously before him.

'The general has told me of your exploits, **shy** servant,' said the emperor. 'I wish to thank you for protecting our people and the wall. You are to move to my palace. You can protect my life.'

Li rose, his **nice** smile beaming like a beacon out to sea. He thought of his departed father. His father would be so proud to see his son in this moment.

❷ **Write a resolution to the climactic scene you wrote in Week 15, Day 5, Question 2 (p.49). Use at least three figures of speech in your scene.**

PERSUASIVE WRITING

Daily checklist

WEEK	DAY 1	DAY 2	DAY 3	DAY 4	DAY 5
17	☐	☐	☐	☐	☐
18	☐	☐	☐	☐	☐
19	☐	☐	☐	☐	☐
20	☐	☐	☐	☐	☐
21	☐	☐	☐	☐	☐
22	☐	☐	☐	☐	☐
23	☐	☐	☐	☐	☐
24	☐	☐	☐	☐	☐

DAY 1

Edit the persuasive piece below by correcting the six subject–verb agreement errors.

THE DANGER OF RELYING ON SUPERHEROES

Fellow unremarkables, we has a problem. The explosive increase in superheroes in recent years has fundamentally changed our way of life, and – dare I say it – not for the better.

Before you come at me with your pitchforks and social media posts, hear me out. I love superheroes. They has done wonderful things for our city and I, like all unremarkables, are grateful for the help they gives us from the goodness of their own hearts. But although good have come from superheroes, their impact have not been altogether positive. I fear that an over-reliance on superheroes, instead of helping us learn to solve our own problems, will put us at more risk than ever before.

DAY 2

! A point of view is an opinion on an issue. An issue is an important topic that people discuss and debate.

1. **Tick the three items that can be defined as issues.**

- ☐ university should be free
- ☐ someone cheats on a school test
- ☐ whether graffiti is an artform
- ☐ how pollination works
- ☐ banning animal testing
- ☐ why streaming is popular

2. **Summarise the point of view expressed in the Day 1 passage above.**

The point of view expressed on the issue of relying on superheroes is ______________________

____.

3. **What is your point of view on this issue?**

If superheroes existed, I think that ______________________________

____.

Daily WRITING & EDITING Practice

DAY 3

Edit the persuasive piece below by correcting the six verb tense errors.

THE POWER OF ART IN THE CLASSROOM

In the context of education, many of us have previously considering art as insignificant – a mere hobby to break up the more serious study of subjects such as science or history. Despite the significant role of art in society, the visual arts have not been given nearly as much attention in schools as they deserve. Recent research will suggest that skills such as drawing and painting can have significant positive effects on our lives, not only during our formative years but also in adulthood. They taught us how to communicate and can also helped with understanding and retaining information.

So I believe it's time we embracing art as an essential part of the national curriculum, teach it with the same rigour and care given to other core subjects.

DAY 4

1. **Summarise, in a single sentence, the point of view in the Day 3 passage above.**

____

2. **Fill in the gaps in the tables below with other issue ideas, then indicate your point of view on each issue by circling 'agree' or 'disagree'.**

School issues	
School uniforms should be mandatory.	POV: agree / disagree
	POV: agree / disagree
	POV: agree / disagree

Environmental issues	
Plastic bags should be banned.	POV: agree / disagree
	POV: agree / disagree
	POV: agree / disagree

DAY 5

1 Edit the persuasive piece below by correcting the three subject–verb agreement errors and the three verb tense errors.

BANNING SMOKING FROM PUBLIC PLACES

We've known for a very long time now that smoking are catastrophic to our health. Tobacco smoke will be full of toxic chemicals that cause harm to the human body. It was also highly addictive, meaning that once you start, it can be very difficult to stop.

Awareness of just how harmful smoking is have grown immensely over the past few decades, and there have been great strides made in reducing the number of people who take up smoking. Yet the harm caused by smoking is deeply significant in our society and, according to the Cancer Council, it is still the leading preventable cause of death in Australia. More must be done to curb the negative effects of smoking. This is why I believes that smoking should be banning from all public places.

2 Provide a point of view for each of the issues below and briefly explain why you feel this way.

a Animal testing should / should not be banned.

____

____

b Graffiti should / should not be considered an artform.

____

____

c Studying at university should / should not be free.

____

____

DAY 1

Edit the persuasive piece below by rewriting the four passive sentences in the active voice. The first two have been done for you.

WHY CARAVANNING IS THE BEST TYPE OF HOLIDAY

The increased affordability of travel and the rise of travel bloggers have transformed the way many of us think about holidays. ~~These days, expensive luxury holidays are considered the most desirable type of vacation.~~ *These days, a lot of people consider expensive luxury holidays to be the most desirable type of vacation.* ~~Glamorous pictures of famous landmarks and popular tourist destinations on social media are demanded by our peers.~~ *Our peers demand glamorous pictures of famous landmarks and popular tourist destinations on our social media.*

But with all this travel mania, we are starting to forget the true purpose of holidaying. We take holidays to escape the monotony of daily life so that we can relax, enjoy ourselves and return refreshed. Our houses don't need to be cleaned every day. The shopping doesn't have to be done weekly. The relaxing nature of caravanning is exactly what makes this one of the best forms of holidaying.

DAY 2

! A contention sums up your point of view on an issue and gives an overall reason for why you hold this view.

1. **Label the following statements as either an issue, a point of view or a contention.**

   I believe that driving tests should be mandatory every year after you turn sixty. ______________________

   Should driving tests be mandatory every year after you turn sixty? ______________________

   Driving tests should be mandatory every year after you turn sixty because people's reflexes can begin to deteriorate from this age. ______________________

2. **Underline a sentence in the Day 1 passage above that expresses the main contention.**

DAY 3

Edit the persuasive piece below by correcting the six punctuation errors (ending punctuation, apostrophes).

COLONISING MARS

Establishing a permanent colony of humans on Mars is not an option; its a necessity because our planet cannot sustain our species forever? The sooner we realise this, the sooner we can set plans in motion to build a better life for future generations.

There are many reason's why humankind must look to outer space for its next home Chief among these is the fact that continued life on Earth is not guaranteed. We must have a backup plan should our planet ever collapse. Furthermore, in the process of developing methods to colonise other planets', our species will make discoveries in science and technology that can improve life on Earth

DAY 4

1. **Summarise, in a single sentence, the argument expressed in the Day 3 passage above.**

   ____

2. **Turn the points of view below into contentions by adding an overall reason that supports the point of view. The first one has been done for you.**

   a **POV:** It should be mandatory to eat vegetables and fruit every day.

   Contention: *It should be mandatory to eat vegetables and fruit every day because they are a good source of vitamins, minerals and dietary fibre.*

   b **POV:** The first lesson of every school day should be exercise.

   Contention: ______________________________

   c **POV:** Every student should go on an exchange program in another country.

   Contention: ______________________________

DAY 5

❶ **Edit the persuasive piece below by rewriting the two passive sentences in the active voice and correcting the two punctuation errors (ending punctuation, apostrophes).**

PROTECTING ENDANGERED SPECIES

These days, it seems as though every other species and their cousin are 'under threat'? The uncomfortable truth is that plants and animals *are* going extinct at an alarming rate. The reason for this is simple: these creatures are being killed by humans.

The impact of human activity such as environmental destruction has made the state of life on Earth incredibly fragile, and the extinction rate is higher than it's been for million's of years. Though it may not seem like it, life on this planet is facing an enormous crisis, and there has never been a more vital time to protect endangered species. Action must be taken now.

❷ **Provide a contention for each of the issues you listed in Week 17, Day 4, Question 2. An example for each type of issue has been provided. Make sure you include an overall reason for why you hold this point of view.**

School issues
School uniforms should be mandatory because they develop a student's sense of belonging and build school spirit.

Environmental issues
Plastic bags should be banned because they do not break down completely and end up harming the environment.

DAY 1

Edit the persuasive piece below by correcting the six spelling errors. **The previous part of this text is on page 55.**

THE DANGER OF RELYING ON SUPERHEROES

In the age of superheroes, our ability to protect ourselves is paramount. Superheroes, much as we don't like to addmit it, are full of weaknesses that can be exploited by villians.

Think about Galactic Cat – a powerful hero who is terriffied of water. Or what about Possum Man, whose tendancy to play dead has led to some sticky situations. Sometimes they will fail, and we must still be able to defend ourselves when they do.

The evils thretening our world are often provoked by the superheroes themselves. Would the evil Captain Vortex have even known about our planet if he hadn't been following Tourist Woman? The destrucsion he caused is a direct result of the actions of a superhero.

DAY 2

To make a contention into an argument, it needs to be reinforced by supporting reasons.

1. **Identify one reason given in the Day 1 passage above to support the main contention.**

___

___

2. **Tick the reason that best supports each of the contentions below.**

a People should stop driving cars because they contribute to pollution.

- ☐ Cars endanger cyclists' lives every day.
- ☐ The exhaust from a car releases carbon dioxide, which contributes to global warming.

b Textbooks are vital for learning and should not be replaced with tablets.

- ☐ Learning from a physical book is shown to help students retain information better than tablets.
- ☐ Tablets are easier to carry around than physical textbooks.

DAY 3

Edit the persuasive piece below by correcting the six apostrophe errors. **The previous part of this text is on page 56.**

THE POWER OF ART IN THE CLASSROOM

We must recognise the many benefits that art, as an educational tool, offer's students. For example, numerous' studies have found strong links between the act of drawing and a persons ability to recall information. As one study explains, the practice of drawing comprise's several element's: memorising an image, using muscle memory to create the work, and forming meaning for the viewer.

Furthermore, art is a highly effective – and often underused – tool for communication. The education system favours written expression, but concept maps, diagram's and illustrations are all effective modes for expressing information.

DAY 4

Fill in the table below with supporting reasons for each side of the issue. The first one has been done for you.

Issue: Should homework be optional?

	FOR	AGAINST
Reason 1	Homework should be optional because it can cause some students anxiety and stress.	Homework shouldn't be optional because it is necessary to help students master key skills.
Reason 2		

Issue: Is life better without computers?

	FOR	AGAINST
Reason 1		
Reason 2		

DAY 5

❶ **Edit the persuasive piece below by correcting the four spelling errors and the four apostrophe errors.** The previous part of this text is on page 57.

BANNING SMOKING FROM PUBLIC PLACES

In addittion to the well-known health disadvantage's of smoking, there are also many social reasons to stop this addictive behaviour. For one, its a very smelly habit. The stench of cigarette smoke lingars on your clothes, as well as on your breathe. Everyone can tell if youre a smoker as soon as you walk into the room, and this may cause them to avoid you. Not only do many people not like to be around those who smoke because of the smell, they also do not want to be exposed to second-hand smoke, which can be very harmful to their health.

Banning smoking from public place's will encourage more people to reduce or completely stop smoking, therebi avoiding the costs to their social life.

❷ **Write a short persuasive piece in response to one of the issues from Week 17, Day 5, Question 2. State your contention clearly and include at least two reasons to support it.**

DAY 1

Edit the persuasive piece below by replacing the words in bold with more interesting or precise adjectives. The previous part of this text is on page 58.

WHY CARAVANNING IS THE BEST TYPE OF HOLIDAY

Caravans may seem an **old** form of travel, but they have many advantages over their flying counterparts. For starters, a road trip is far more comfortable than an aeroplane flight. In a caravan, you don't have to worry about airsick passengers, **clumsy** bathroom line-ups, or **bad** children kicking the back of your seat.

A caravan holiday is also much cheaper than a plane ticket. Instead of spending years saving for one **quick** journey, all you need is a spare weekend and a few litres of petrol.

Finally, the environmental benefits of caravanning are undeniable. Aeroplanes require **giant** amounts of fuel and, according to Forbes.com, are one of the **biggest** contributors of carbon emissions in the world.

DAY 2

! Evidence is used to back up reasons, and can include facts, statistics, quotes and examples.

1 Label the types of evidence below as either fact, statistic, quote or example.

a Universal health care is a system that provides quality medical services to all citizens, regardless of their ability to pay. ______________

b Dr Carissa F Etienne says, 'Universal health coverage means healthier societies and communities.' ______________

c I was hospitalised in America and had to pay $60 000 because I was uninsured. ______________

d A 10% increase in health spending per capita is associated with a gain of 3.5 months of life expectancy. ______________

2 Underline one piece of evidence in the Day 1 passage above and explain how it supports the reason presented.

____

DAY 3

Edit the persuasive piece below by rewriting the three passive sentences in the active voice.
The previous part of this text is on page 59.

COLONISING MARS

History shows us that surviving as a species on this infinitesimal rock we call home is difficult and by no means guaranteed. We only need to look as far back as the age of dinosaurs to see this. Earth was roamed by dinosaurs for over 165 million years. And yet, these fearsome creatures were completely wiped out by a colossal asteroid.

That is why we need to become a multi-planet species. Life is volatile, and the only guarantees are the ones we make for ourselves. In time, Mars will be viewed by future generations as a second home.

DAY 4

Fill in the mind map to complete the plan for a persuasive piece. (You may choose to research appropriate evidence to support your reason.)

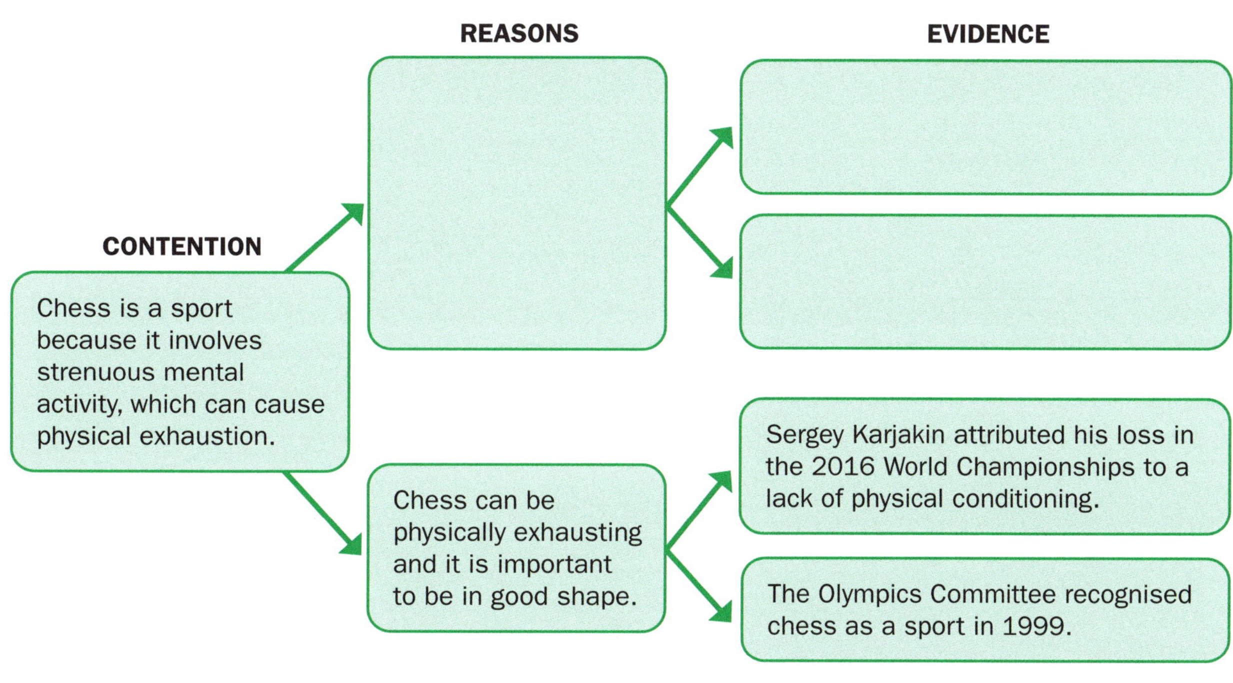

Daily WRITING & EDITING Practice

DAY 5

❶ **Edit the persuasive piece below by replacing the words in bold with more interesting or precise adjectives and rewriting the two passive sentences in the active voice.** **The previous part of this text is on page 60.**

PROTECTING ENDANGERED SPECIES

Too many species are being made endangered or extinct by us. In 2019, *ABC News* reported that the number of species that became extinct in the twentieth century would have taken between 800 and 10 000 years to become extinct without the influence of human activity. That's a **large** difference.

Statistics like these are why many **loved** scientists believe that we are currently living through what is called the Holocene extinction; that is, a mass extinction driven by humans in which species are dying out at a much faster rate than is natural. To put things in perspective, the last mass extinction occurred when the dinosaurs were obliterated by an asteroid collision.

❷ **Write a short persuasive piece in response to one of the issues you brainstormed in Week 17, Day 5, Question 2. Include at least three pieces of evidence to support your reasons.**

___

___

___

___

___

___

___

___

___

DAY 1

Edit the persuasive piece below by correcting the three run-on sentences. **The previous part of this text is on page 61.**

THE DANGER OF RELYING ON SUPERHEROES

Even worse than the fallibility of superheroes, or the potential dangers they bring, is the threat they pose to our attitudes as a society. Unremarkables, our very independence is at stake, we must change our behaviour now!

With so much superpowered help available, I've been seeing a concerning shift in people's behaviour over the past few years, so many times, I see civilians choosing to simply wait for help to come to them instead of solving their own problems. We cannot rely on the kindness of a superhero every time a cat gets stuck in a tree, we need ladders, not charitable, sometimes obnoxious crusaders who can fly.

DAY 2

Persuasive texts are written in language that is carefully selected by the writer to evoke particular emotions in the intended audience.

Write a sentence using each of the following persuasive techniques for one of the issues you wrote down in Week 17, Day 4, Question 2.

	Example 1 – Life is not better without computers.	**Example 2 –** ______
Anecdote – a short, personal story	Yesterday my computer broke down. I couldn't do my homework, chat with friends or stream any films. It was like I was living in the Dark Ages.	
Appeal to fear – makes the audience feel afraid	More and more jobs are centred around technology. Without computers, students like us will fall behind and struggle to get a job after school.	
Rhetorical question – a question that does not require an answer	Can you imagine living in a world where you can't look up information instantly? Or be able to order items online at the touch of a button?	

Daily WRITING & EDITING Practice

DAY 3

Edit the persuasive piece below by correcting the five plural errors. **The previous part of this text is on page 62.**

THE POWER OF ART IN THE CLASSROOM

While art makes an important contribution to education, it also retains value long after student leave school. Most of us, after school or university, never use our skills in differentiating fractions or writing timed essay. But the ability to use drawing and painting as tool for both learning and communication – as well as emotional and interpersonal expression – remains relevant. Visual art offers alternative ways of viewing, organising, understanding and presenting informations, encouraging us to embrace – rather than suppress – individual expression. And yet, how many adults and young adults are so stifled by 'academic' curricula that they refuse to ever pick up a paintbrushes once they finish their schooling?

DAY 4

Write a sentence using each of the following persuasive techniques for one of the issues you brainstormed in Week 17, Day 4, Question 2.

	Example 1 – Children should not have to sit exams.	**Example 2 –** ________
Appeal to a sense of justice – based on people's idea of fairness	It is unfair to make young people sit exams. Exams not only induce stress and anxiety, but they also disadvantage more creative and tactile learners.	
Inclusive language – using pronouns such as 'we' and 'us'	We must all act to stop the injustice of standardised testing. It is up to all of us to make our educators see the error of their ways.	
Repetition – using a word or phrase several times	Does any child deserve to face the pressures of exams? Does any child deserve to feel scared of failure?	

DAY 5

❶ **Edit the persuasive piece below by correcting the three run-on sentences and the three plural errors.** **The previous part of this text is on page 63.**

BANNING SMOKING FROM PUBLIC PLACES

Smoking isn't just bad for your health – it's terrible for the environment, too. Have you ever taken a stroll through a park, only to find the ground coated with squashed-out cigarette butt, with cigarette butts the most common litter item in our country, this is far from an unusual experience. Apart from their ugly sight and smell, cigarette butts are dangerous, the toxic chemicals in abandoned cigarettes can go on to directly damage the environments.

Keeping smoking confined to private space can help reduce the amount of environmental damage caused by cigarettes, it can also reduce the horrid sight of grey smoke floating up into our clear, clean sky.

❷ **Fill in the gaps using one of the persuasive techniques listed on pages 67 and 68.**

All students should go on exchange to another country because it gives them experiences they might not otherwise encounter. Firstly, it means they get to live away from home. ____

________________. Secondly, it teaches them to be more responsible because they have to survive without the daily support of their parents or families. ________________

____.

Thirdly, if they go to a country that speaks a different language from their native tongue, they will pick up that language through their daily interactions with fellow students and other people in the community. ______________________________

____.

DAY 1

Edit the persuasive piece below by correcting the seven verb tense errors. **The previous part of this text is on page 64.**

WHY CARAVANNING IS THE BEST TYPE OF HOLIDAY

Caravans were all well and good, you may say, but where can they actually take you? Well, the answer to that will be – anywhere! We in Australia will have the good fortune to live on a continent of our own, with a huge swathe of land just wait to be explored. You'd be surprised at the number of self-proclaimed globe-trotting Aussies who have never even bothering to visit their neighbouring state!

What's more, as a domestic traveller you were contributing to small, local communities rather than help out huge multinational tourist companies. With our unique wildlife and environmental marvels, why would you go anywhere else?

DAY 2

The primary purpose of persuasive language is to position the audience to agree with your point of view.

1. **Underline a persuasive technique in the passage above and explain how it helps the writer to position the audience to agree with their point of view.**

____

____

2. **Match the short passages below to the persuasive technique being used.**

Passage	Technique
It is very wrong that people are being punished for protesting. No matter the issue, every citizen has a right to express their opinion.	appeal to fear
Can we really afford to have big overseas corporations come in and set up shop in our small community? What will happen to our local businesses, to our jobs, to our way of life?	anecdote
I had to take my elderly mother to the hospital today. We had to wait for hours; it was so crowded. This just shows how much our health sector needs help.	appeal to a sense of justice

DAY **3**

Edit the persuasive piece below by rewriting the three passive sentences in the active voice.
The previous part of this text is on page 65.

COLONISING MARS

The lessons learned from space exploration can be used by us in many ways. Take for example NASA's prized Hubble Space Telescope. Engineers had to design a computer algorithm to extract information from the blurry images taken by the telescope. They shared this algorithm with a doctor who applied it to the X-ray images he was taking to detect breast cancer. The discovery that the algorithm did a better job of detecting early stages of breast cancer than the method used at the time was made by this doctor.

Potential life-changing discoveries that can be applied by us to other facets of human life are limitless.

DAY **4**

State which of the passages below you think is most effective in persuading an audience and explain why.

a I think children should be allowed to play video games. I played video games all the time growing up, and I don't think they're a waste of time. Even though it means spending hours staring at a screen, it doesn't matter because video games are fun.

b There are many reasons why video games are beneficial to children. For a start, they help with real-world problem solving. Playing *SimCity* as a child taught me how to plan and lay out a city, and now I'm an urban planner. Why wouldn't we want children to have fun and learn while they do so?

Explanation: ____

____

DAY 5

1 **Edit the persuasive piece below by correcting the two verb tense errors and rewriting the two passive sentences in the active voice.** **The previous part of this text is on page 66.**

PROTECTING ENDANGERED SPECIES

The horrific consequences of pollution, habitat destruction and, of course, climate change are swept under the rug time and time again. What do our actions saying about our values as a species?

We need to end these shortcomings of human action now. A huge impact on the health of the environment can be made by the loss of just one species. As the Endangered Species Coalition will put it, 'without healthy forests, grasslands, rivers, oceans and other ecosystems, we will not have clean air, water, or land'. The plants and animals that inhabit these areas must stop being endangered by us.

2 **Write a short persuasive piece on a topic of your choice. Include at least three persuasive techniques targeted at your intended audience.**

DAY 1

Edit the persuasive piece below by correcting the six punctuation errors (commas, apostrophes). **The previous part of this text is on page 67.**

THE DANGER OF RELYING ON SUPERHEROES

While its true that our planet has never been under so much protection it has also never been under greater threat. Now is not the time to allow ourselves to be at the mercy of anyone, with powers.

Unremarkables, we are not helpless! We may not be able to fly or crush our enemies' with our minds, but we can be just as courageous and heroic as any 'Captain this' or 'Commander that'. And we must be, vigilant. We can no longer sit idly by and wait to be rescued. Its time we put our efforts into aiding superheroes in their fight against evil, for the good of the world and the dignity of us as a people.

DAY 2

In addition to including the main elements of a persuasive text, a text for presentation must be written with purpose, audience and tone in mind.

1. **Who is the intended audience for the speech above?**

   ____

2. **What does the writer want to achieve with this speech? Do you think they achieve this purpose?**

   ____

   ____

3. **Match the audience and purpose to the most appropriate language description.**

Announcement from a leading doctor encouraging children to eat five servings of fruit and vegetables a day	emotional, begging
Social media post scolding people who carelessly litter in public	serious, reasonable
Email from an activist group asking young people to protest the inhumane treatment of animals in zoos	aggressive, bossy

DAY 3

Edit the persuasive piece below by correcting the five capitalisation errors. **The previous part of this text is on page 68.**

THE POWER OF ART IN THE CLASSROOM

mrs jaspers, fellow classmates, let's imagine a world where art is given the same level of respect as science, english and mathematics. A world in which students are encouraged to visualise as well as verbalise their learning, and are equipped with the skills to do so. A world in which visual learners are not left behind in text-heavy subjects, and where adults in all fields are able and free to convey their ideas in ways beyond the limitations of the written word.

Art is a tool to be harnessed for the purposes of teaching, expression and communication. It should not be confined to the elitist world of galleries and museums. it deserves a vibrant, active role in all areas of our society and at all stages of life, and this begins in the Classroom.

DAY 4

❶ **Circle the word below that best describes the tone of the passage above.**

sorrowful | hostile | passionate

❷ **How does the tone help the writer to achieve their purpose?**

____

____

❸ **Replace each word in bold below with a word that has a more positive connotation (the associated meanings of a word). The first one has been done for you.**

a You need to be **pushy** _assertive_ when you are looking for a job.

b Mr Miller is a **weird** __________________ teacher.

c My sister likes to save her money; she is really **cheap** __________________ .

d Albus is a very **naughty** __________________ student.

Daily WRITING & EDITING Practice

DAY 5

❶ **Edit the persuasive piece below by correcting the four punctuation errors (commas, apostrophes) and the four capitalisation errors.** **The previous part of this text is on page 69.**

BANNING SMOKING FROM PUBLIC PLACES

over the year's, we have made great leaps, in reducing the popularity of smoking, but more can still be done – and should be done. The way forward is clear. all public area's must become smoke-free to protect us, from the harmful effects of tobacco smoke, to protect the environment from toxic chemicals in discarded cigarettes and to discourage others from taking up this dangerous habit.

Most people would agree that the fewer people who take up smoking, the better. If you agree, i implore you to pressure your government to ban smoking from all public areas and join me in my fight to create a healthier, smoke-free Society.

❷ **Complete the following planning sheet for a speech to present to your class.**

Issue	
Main contention	
Purpose	
Audience	
Tone	
Reason 1	
Reason 1 evidence	
Reason 2	
Reason 2 evidence	

DAY 1

Edit the persuasive piece below by adding six linking words or phrases. The first three have been done for you. The previous part of this text is on page 70.

WHY CARAVANNING IS THE BEST TYPE OF HOLIDAY

Holidaying *, as we know,* is one of the greatest joys of the modern world. ~~Before~~ *But before* we head off to the next destination, we must stop and consider three things: *firstly,* we must consider our past, a time when holidaying meant a relaxing escape rather than a race to tick tourism hotspots off a bucket list; we must consider our present and learn to appreciate the beautiful land at our doorstep, while supporting local communities; we must consider our future and refuse to participate in the environmental destruction caused by air travel. Caravan holidays truly are the best type of holiday, and they are more crucial now than ever before.

DAY 2

> There are several persuasive techniques that are particularly effective in a speech, including repetition, inclusive language and rhetorical questions.

1. **Underline one use of repetition in the passage above and explain its effect in persuading the audience.**

   ____

   ____

2. **Underline one or more uses of inclusive language in the passage above and explain its effect in persuading the audience.**

   ____

   ____

3. **Write a short opening for a speech (on an issue of your choice) that immediately engages the audience.**

   ____

   ____

   ____

DAY 3

Edit the persuasive piece below by correcting the six punctuation errors (commas, ending punctuation). **The previous part of this text is on page 71.**

COLONISING MARS

Fellow earthlings we have often regarded space colonisation as a distant dream, but it is time to stop dreaming and make other planetary settlement, a reality for future generations? Famed astrophysicist Stephen Hawking said it best: 'If the human race is to continue for another million years, we will have to boldly go where no-one has gone before?'

Make no mistake – this endeavour will take time and considerable investment of resources. If we begin a plan to establish a colony on Mars, we won't see the fruits of our labour, for at least a hundred years. But is that not what we must do to secure the future of our species

DAY 4

1. **Underline the rhetorical question in the passage above and explain its effect in persuading the audience.**

___

___

2. **State which speech opening you find more compelling and explain why.**

   a We, the children of tomorrow, are presented with an opportunity to bring about positive change. We, the children of tomorrow, can help those less fortunate than ourselves. We, the children of tomorrow, can bring about tomorrow, today.

   b There is so much that children can offer society. Children are clever, resourceful, passionate and full of hope. They have many new and exciting ideas. Whatever they come up with, it should be quite exciting.

___

___

DAY 5

❶ **Edit the persuasive piece below by adding four linking words or phrases and correcting the four punctuation errors (commas, ending punctuation).** **The previous part of this text is on page 72.**

PROTECTING ENDANGERED SPECIES

It is no secret that the health of our planet is deteriorating. The effects of human activity on the natural world, include contamination and destruction, and we are at a tipping point. There are several ways we can help make up for our predecessors' actions? We need to look after all life forms on this planet. We need to put more effort into conserving endangered species. And lastly, we need to end the mistreatment of the environment that causes their endangerment in the first place.

Repairing the damage may not seem possible. If we had the power to cause it surely we also have the power to fix it, and we owe it to ourselves, our children and the planet to try

❷ **Write the introduction to a speech on a persuasive issue of your choice. Remember to include persuasive techniques that will appeal to your intended audience.**

Issue: ______________________________

Intended audience: ______________________________

____

____

____

____

____

____

____

____

____

INFORMATIVE WRITING

UNIT 4

Daily checklist

WEEK	DAY 1	DAY 2	DAY 3	DAY 4	DAY 5
25	☐	☐	☐	☐	☐
26	☐	☐	☐	☐	☐
27	☐	☐	☐	☐	☐
28	☐	☐	☐	☐	☐
29	☐	☐	☐	☐	☐
30	☐	☐	☐	☐	☐
31	☐	☐	☐	☐	☐
32	☐	☐	☐	☐	☐

DAY 1

Edit the informative piece below by correcting the six spelling errors.

ALL ABOUT VOLCANOES

Did you know that there are more then twenty volcanoes erupting around the world at this very moment? There are around 1500 active volcanoes on Earth, and many more dormant and extinct ones (those that haven't erupted in over 10 000 years).

In order to know how volcanoes erupt, it helps to understand how they form. The Earth is made up of hundreds of tetonic plates that form the top layer of the planet's crust. These plates can move around and colide, which causes some of the melted rock below to rise up and make a volcano.

Although volcanoes may seem frightening, volcanic eruptions from long ago formed many islands, beautiful mountans and pristin lakes that we appreciate today.

DAY 2

Informative writing conveys factual information about a topic, without presenting a strong opinion on it.

1. **Tick four topics below that could be turned into informative texts.**

- [ ] How a solar eclipse works
- [ ] A story about a vampire
- [ ] Should voting be compulsory?
- [ ] How laws are passed
- [ ] An analysis of *Frozen 2*
- [ ] Boxing should be illegal
- [ ] Explaining dreams
- [ ] A history of the Olympic Games

2. **How does informative writing differ from persuasive writing?**

____

____

____

____

DAY 3

Edit the informative piece below by correcting the four subject–verb agreement errors.

THE ORIGINS OF THE CHINESE ZODIAC

The Chinese zodiac are a popular astrology system in China consisting of a cycle of twelve animals: Rat, Ox, Tiger, Rabbit, Dragon, Snake, Horse, Goat, Monkey, Rooster, Dog and Pig. Each animal correspond with a particular year on the Chinese lunar calendar, and every twelve years the cycle start again, beginning with the Rat.

The animal representing the year that a person is born are thought to determine certain aspects of their personality, according to the characteristics associated with the animal. For example, someone born in the year of the Rat might be thought to be quick-witted and clever, while someone born in the year of the Ox might be thought to be stubborn and loyal.

DAY 4

Brainstorm informative topic ideas using the categories below as a guide. An example for each category has been provided.

NATURE	HISTORY	SOCIETY
The lives of ants	The formation of the United Nations	The evolution of teenage slang
TECHNOLOGY	**EDUCATION**	**SCIENCE**
How to create a TikTok video	The first university in the world	Design of miniature robots based on insects

DAY 5

1 Edit the informative piece below by correcting the three spelling errors and the three subject–verb agreement errors.

THE RISE OF REALITY TV

The Voice. MasterChef. The Bachalor. The Masked Singer. Next Top Model. The list goes on and on. These types of shows dominates airwaves and are the topic of conversation in many households across the country. But were reality TV series always as popular as they are now?

While unscripted series following real-life people and celebrities has existed for many decades, it wasn't until the early 2000s that the genre really exploded. Now we can't turn on our televisions without seeing contestants blabbing to a camera as they share their innemost thoughts and deepest, darkest secrets with the whole world.

The metoric rise of reality TV have had a profound impact on our society, shifting our collective interest from current events to the exploits of the Kardashian clan and farmers looking for wives.

2 Write three interesting questions for the topic below. The first one has been done for you. Then write three interesting questions for one of the topics you brainstormed in Day 4.

Topic 1: All about dwarf planets

Question 1: *Why did Pluto get reassigned as a dwarf planet?*

Question 2: ____________________

Question 3: ____________________

Topic 2: ____________________

Question 1: ____________________

Question 2: ____________________

Question 3: ____________________

Daily WRITING & EDITING Practice

DAY 1

Edit the informative piece below by combining each pair of underlined sentences.

THE LARGEST APE THAT EVER LIVED

Gigantopithecus was a type of ape. It lived in the forests of Southeast Asia for millions of years. It became extinct around 100 000 years ago during what is known as the Pleistocene epoch. As the name suggests, *Gigantopithecus* was massive – it was almost twice as tall as the average adult human and is the largest primate to have ever walked the Earth.

Luckily for any ancient humans that might have been around at the time, the enormous ape is thought to have been a herbivore. It would only have eaten plants. These include bamboo and fruit.

DAY 2

Informative texts aim to present readers with information about a specific topic, so it is important to research a topic thoroughly, using reliable sources, before beginning to write.

❶ Tick the three best methods for researching an informative topic.

- ☐ asking your best friend
- ☐ guessing
- ☐ searching on the internet
- ☐ calling a psychic
- ☐ asking an expert
- ☐ reading books

❷ Using one of the methods you ticked above, research and answer the three questions you devised for your topic in Week 25, Day 5, Question 2.

Answer 1: ______________________________

____

Answer 2: ______________________________

____

Answer 3: ______________________________

____

DAY 3

Edit the informative piece below by replacing the words in bold with more interesting and precise adjectives.

THE ORIGINS OF THE MĀORI LANGUAGE

Kia ora! If you've ever heard this greeting before, you have most likely been to **fine** New Zealand. But what language does it come from? *Kia ora* is a way to say hello in Māori, a language also known as 'te reo'. Māori is the language spoken by the Māori people, the indigenous population of New Zealand. However, if you travelled north to the Cook Islands, you would hear a slightly **diverse** greeting: *kia orana*. And if you travelled further north still, all the way to **pretty** Tahiti, you would hear the Tahitian greeting *la orana* (pronounced yo-rah-nah).

These eastern Polynesian languages have a **flavourful** history and, although they have evolved over time, they continue to be important to the identity of those who speak them.

DAY 4

Research three interesting facts about the topic below. An example is provided as a guide.

Topic	Fact 1	Fact 2	Fact 3
The history of Valentine's Day	St Valentine performed secret marriages in defiance of Roman Emperor Claudius II's orders. He was executed on 14 February 269 for his disobedience.	The oldest record of a valentine was a poem that Charles, Duke of Orléans, wrote to his wife when he was imprisoned in the Tower of London in 1415.	In the late Middle Ages, young men and women drew names to see who their valentine would be.
The role of cats throughout history			

DAY 5

❶ **Edit the informative piece below by combining each pair of underlined sentences and replacing the words in bold with more interesting and precise adjectives.**

THE ROLE OF ARTIFICIAL INTELLIGENCE

Once just an idea in science fiction stories, 'artificial intelligence', or AI, has come to attract **important** attention over the years. <u>It was first classified as a science in 1955. It has grown rapidly as a field of study since then.</u>

But what exactly is AI? This can be very subjective – ask three experts and you're likely to get four different answers. Broadly speaking, AI refers to an idea proposed by the **smart** mathematician Alan Turing in 1950: can machines think? <u>The goal of AI is to create machines that are able to perceive, process and learn. This is similar to the way people function.</u>

❷ **Research an interesting fact for each of the ancient civilisations below. One fact has been provided for each as a guide.**

Civilisation	Facts
Ancient Greece	**Fact 1:** In ancient Greece, a unibrow was considered a sign of intelligence and great beauty in women. **Fact 2:** ______________________
Ancient Egypt	**Fact 1:** Ancient Egyptians, who weren't afraid to protest for better working conditions, organised one of the first recorded strikes in history. **Fact 2:** ______________________
Maya	**Fact 1:** Mayans played a game that involved hitting a ball through a hoop. It was similar to basketball, except that you couldn't use your hands and feet to score points. **Fact 2:** ______________________

DAY 1

Edit the informative piece below by rewriting the three passive sentences in the active voice.
The previous part of this text is on page 81.

ALL ABOUT VOLCANOES

Volcanoes can be found on every continent and come in many different shapes and sizes. They are found interesting by many of us. The melted rock inside a volcano is called magma, and when it leaves the volcano it's called lava. Though it is very hot and dangerous, the lava eventually cools down and turns back into rock. Layers on a volcano are formed by this rock.

Volcanic eruptions can create calderas, which look like empty lakes on the top of a mountain. Famous calderas in Yellowstone National Park, United States, and Santorini, Greece, are visited by tourists every year.

DAY 2

Sort the topics below into the most appropriate organisational category: chronological (in order of time), sequential (steps or progression) or cause and effect (one event causing the next). Then add one topic of your own for each category.

It is important to present ideas in a logical way that helps readers understand the information being presented.

Why oil spills happen | A history of women's right to vote | How electricity works | How laws are created | Effects of a vegan diet | How Google began

Chronological	Sequential	Cause and effect

Daily WRITING & EDITING Practice

DAY 3

Edit the informative piece below by correcting the six verb tense errors. The previous part of this text is on page 82.

THE ORIGINS OF THE CHINESE ZODIAC

The Chinese zodiac will have a very long history in China. There are many myths and stories that try to explain the origins of the zodiac. One of the most famous tells the story of a great race between the animals, organising by an ancient god called the Jade Emperor. The order in which the animals won the race becomes their position in the twelve-year cycle.

Although the exact beginnings of the Chinese zodiac will not be recorded, many historians believe that the animal symbols were first used by Chinese people during the Han dynasty (206 BC to 220 AD). Some people believe that the lunar calendar, which can be trace back to the fourteenth century BC, paves the way for the sequence of the zodiac animals.

DAY 4

1. **Which organisational approach is being used in the Day 3 passage above? Explain whether or not you think this approach supports the purpose of this topic and why.**

____

____

____

2. **Select an organisational approach for one of the topics you brainstormed in Week 25, Day 4. Explain how this approach supports the purpose of this topic.**

Topic: _______________________________________

Organisational approach: ______________________

Explanation: __________________________________

____

____

DAY 5

❶ **Edit the informative piece below by rewriting the three passive sentences in the active voice and correcting the three verb tense errors.** **The previous part of this text is on page 83.**

THE RISE OF REALITY TV

Arguably, the culture of 'look at me' television begins with *Survivor* and *Big Brother*. Premiere in 2000 in the United States, the two series were essentially game shows; however, they also doubled as experiments in human responses and interactions. These series were watched by millions of viewers. The drama of emotional breakdowns of contestants and choosing who to cheer for was what attracted such big audiences. This appeal is never more evident than in series like *The Bachelor* and *The Bachelorette*. These will have many symbols of romance, such as candles and roses. But what leaves viewers wanting more are the weekly eliminations showing close-ups of broken-hearted contestants.

❷ **Write a short introduction for one of the topics you brainstormed in Week 25, Day 4. Remember to structure your piece according to one of the organisational categories.**

DAY 1

Edit the informative piece below by correcting the eight capitalisation errors. **The previous part of this text is on page 84.**

THE LARGEST APE THAT EVER LIVED

According to Science writer colin Barras, *Gigantopithecus* was officially discovered in 1935, when a german anthropologist named ralph von Koenigswald found an enormous fossilised tooth in a pharmacy in Hong Kong. It was being sold as a 'dragon tooth', a common name for fossils used in traditional chinese medicine.

For such an enormous creature, you'd think there would be plenty of fossilised bones left to discover. However, since von Koenigswald identified that first tooth, scientists have only found a few thousand teeth and some jawbone fragments, mostly from caves in southern China. as barras writes, porcupines might be to blame. porcupines chew on bones for calcium, and it is likely that they 'ate most of the evidence for the world's biggest ape'.

DAY 2

! Before you start writing an informative text, creating an outline and considering your purpose can help you decide which facts to include.

1. **Tick the fact below that best supports the purpose of the topic.**

   Topic: Common uses of hypnosis

   Purpose: To educate people about the benefits of hypnosis

   ☐ Hypnosis can be used to make people do embarrassing things.

   ☐ Hypnosis can help people trace the source of and overcome their fears.

2. **Research two facts that support the purpose of the topic below.**

   Topic: The evolution of teenage slang

   Purpose: To show how teenage slang has changed over time

   - Fact 1: ______________________________
   - Fact 2: ______________________________

DAY 3

Edit the informative piece below by adding three linking words or phrases. **The previous part of this text is on page 85.**

THE ORIGINS OF THE MĀORI LANGUAGE

The Māori language is rich and varied. In the same way that Australian English differs from American English, Māori has slight variations depending on location. The Cook Islands are made up of fifteen islands spread over a large area. Some islands are very difficult to reach, so the people on these different islands started using different pronunciations, and sometimes completely different words. When the Māori people settled in New Zealand, their language changed again.

The various dialects of Māori were originally spoken languages, which means there was no way to write them down. The Māori people used traditional songs, dances, carvings and weavings to pass on messages.

DAY 4

1. **Cross out two sentences in the informative passage below that do not support the specified purpose.**

   Topic: The role of dreams **Purpose:** To explain the various functions of dreaming

   Dreams are hallucinations that occur during certain stages of sleep. Some people argue that you cannot dream while you are snoring. Though scientists don't entirely agree on the purpose of dreams, there are several widely held beliefs. The main theory is that dreams help us to confront emotional traumas in our life. Interestingly, people who are born blind still have dreams, even though they do not see visuals in their dreams. Another popular theory is that dreams help us to sort through complicated thoughts and feelings.

2. **Explain why you made the choices you did.**

   ____

   ____

DAY 5

❶ **Edit the informative piece below by correcting the two capitalisation errors and adding two linking words or phrases.** **The previous part of this text is on page 86.**

THE ROLE OF ARTIFICIAL INTELLIGENCE

one implementation of AI you might be familiar with is the development of computer programs to master various games. A famous example is Deep Blue, a supercomputer that beat former chess world champion garry Kasparov in 1997. The program AlphaZero managed to master games such as chess, after being given nothing but the rules, in just under four hours. It was tested against other AI programs and won convincingly. Many people couldn't master noughts-and-crosses in that time!

There are plans to incorporate AI into gameplay to an even greater extent. This would enable games to change and respond to player feedback.

❷ **Complete an outline for one of the topics you brainstormed in Week 25, Day 4.**

TOPIC:

PURPOSE OF THE PIECE:

SENTENCE INTRODUCING THE TOPIC:

INTERESTING FACT 1:

INTERESTING FACT 2:

CONCLUDING STATEMENT:

DAY 1

Edit the informative piece below by correcting the six punctuation errors (ending punctuation, semicolons). The previous part of this text is on page 87.

ALL ABOUT VOLCANOES

How a volcano erupts depends on its shape, size and type of magma? Imagine opening a bottle of soft drink and pouring some into a glass the liquid would flow out of the bottle easily and, hopefully, not make a mess. Now, imagine that you shook that bottle before you opened it gas would build up and cause the liquid to explode out, spraying everywhere..

The same thing happens in a volcano. If the magma inside is runny, there is less gas in it that needs to escape, and the lava will flow out slowly If the magma is thick and full of gas, there can be an explosive eruption; sending ash and magma high into the air.

DAY 2

Expanding on ideas with detail and description helps to add depth and interest to informative texts.

Complete the table below by researching and expanding on the facts for each topic. The first one has been done for you.

Topic	Fact	Additional description
History of the US flag	The current flag of the United States was designed by a high-school student in 1958.	Bob Heft received a B for his History project. After President Dwight D Eisenhower chose Heft's design, the B was upgraded to an A.
Interesting national animals	The unicorn is the national animal of Scotland.	
Zombie ants	The *Ophiocordyceps unilateralis* fungus infects a foraging ant and slowly alters its behaviour.	

Daily WRITING & EDITING Practice

DAY 3

Edit the informative piece below by joining each pair of underlined sentences. **The previous part of this text is on page 88.**

THE ORIGINS OF THE CHINESE ZODIAC

The true origin of the Chinese zodiac is much more difficult to ascertain. According to one online museum, there are legends that suggest the Chinese calendar was created by Emperor Huangdi in 2637 BC. The zodiac animals were thought to have become attached to the calendar much later. The exact date is unknown. The earliest artefacts featuring the animals emerged during the Warring States period in ancient China (475–221 BC). Exactly where and how these zodiac animals were first created is still contested among scholars. Over time, the zodiac spread from China across Asia. Many different Asian countries have their own version of the twelve zodiac animals.

DAY 4

Annotate the informative poster below with added description for each fact.

HISTORY OF AMUSEMENT PARKS

1903 New York's Luna Park was founded in 1903 and served as a stand-in for world travel. Patrons could take a tour of mock versions of countries such as India, Japan and Ireland. →

1895 The first permanent enclosed amusement park was opened in Coney Island, Brooklyn, USA, in 1895. →

1800s The invention of mechanical rides in the late 1800s led to amusement parks as we know them. But, before that, pleasure gardens and world fairs had a similar purpose. →

DAY 5

1 **Edit the informative piece below by correcting the two punctuation errors (ending punctuation, semicolons) and joining each pair of underlined sentences.** **The previous part of this text is on page 89.**

THE RISE OF REALITY TV

There are people who don't religiously follow the lives of reality TV contestants. These people often wonder what the appeal of the genre is. 'What is so fascinating about the lives of complete strangers and celebrities?' they ask? 'How can people delight in the tears and triumphs of people they don't personally know?' they muse.

Reality TV series remain very popular today. They tap into our desire to see ordinary people on the screen. Media psychiatrist and reality television consultant Dr Carole Lieberman explains; 'We live vicariously through the experiences of the reality TV stars from the safety of our own homes.'

2 **Using the plan below, write a body paragraph for one of the topics you brainstormed in Week 25, Day 4.**

Topic sentence/interesting fact: ____________________

____

____

Explanation/added detail: ____________________

____

____

____

Summary sentence: ____________________

____

DAY 1

Edit the informative piece below by correcting the four subject–verb agreement errors.
The previous part of this text is on page 90.

THE LARGEST APE THAT EVER LIVED

So, what happened to *Gigantopithecus*? While the giant ape might have seemed indestructible, some scientists believes that its enormous size may have ultimately been its downfall – fossils indicate it stood as high as three metres and weighed up to 500 kilograms. Aaron Clauset, a computer scientist at the University of Boulder, explains that 'being bigger ... brings long-term risk'.

As *National Geographic* report, larger animals requires greater amounts of food. They also usually has fewer offspring than smaller animals. This turned out to be a fatal combination for *Gigantopithecus* when a sudden change in climate was caused by an ice age. Unlike smaller apes – such as its closest living relative, the orangutan – *Gigantopithecus* simply couldn't adapt quickly enough to survive its new environment.

DAY 2

! The use of definitions, statistics, quotes and studies adds authority and detail to informative texts.

1. **Underline one piece of evidence in the passage above.**
2. **How does this piece of evidence strengthen the passage?**

   ____

   ____

3. **Research an interesting fact about *Gigantopithecus* not mentioned in the Day 1 passage above, and support it with one piece of evidence.**

   ____

   ____

   ____

DAY 3

Edit the informative piece below by correcting the six spelling errors. **The previous part of this text is on page 91.**

THE ORIGINS OF THE MĀORI LANGUAGE

The Māori language was affected when English settlers arrived in New Zealand in 1769. On borde James Cook's ship was a Tahitian high cheif who was able to translate between Cook and the Māori people, since the Polynesian languages were similar to Māori. But as the English people learned the local language and started to right it down, so that they could document sales and ownership, several English words were integrated into the Māori language. Though it was thretened and nearly disappeared over time, *te reo* was listed as an oficial New Zealand language in 1987, and many restaration projects are aimed at preserving it.

DAY 4

Answer the questions below with evidence-based facts. The first one has been done for you.

a Are there active volcanoes on the moon?

While there are currently no active volcanoes on the moon, recent NASA findings suggest that there may have been lava flow from active volcanoes around 100 million years ago.

b Have humans jumped further than horses at the Olympics? ________________

____

c Can bees fly higher than Mount Everest? ________________

____

d Are peanuts a type of nut? ________________

____

DAY 5

❶ **Edit the informative piece below by correcting the three subject–verb agreement errors and the three spelling errors.** The previous part of this text is on page 92.

THE ROLE OF ARTIFICIAL INTELLIGENCE

A prominant example of the influence AI could potentially have on our lives are self-driving cars. The day in which all cars are self-driving may not be as far away as you might think. The basis of all of this development have been the advances in artificial intelligence. The systems driving cars have to be 'trained' to percieve and react to all sorts of information – think about the shear number of factors that could affect a car ride. Estimates are that a self-driving vehicle in 2020 could contain as much as 300 million lines of code, and be expected to process stimuli at a ridiculous speed. But just imagine being able to relax and watch your favourite TV show while the car you're in do all the work for you!

❷ **Write an informative paragraph on one of the topics below. Support your researched facts with at least two pieces of evidence.**

- The emergence of streaming services, such as Netflix
- A social media platform, such as TikTok

DAY 1

Edit the informative piece below by correcting the six verb tense errors. **The previous part of this text is on page 93.**

ALL ABOUT VOLCANOES

While there are thousands of volcanoes around the world, some are more famous than others. Mount Vesuvius, a stratovolcano in Italy, will be known for its explosive eruption in 79 AD, which destroys several Roman cities, including Pompeii. The cities are preserved by being buried in the rock and ash thrown from the volcano, and volcanologists have been able to learn about how people live back then by studying the remains.

A famous shield volcano, called Kīlauea, can be found in Hawaii. This volcano continuously erupting from 1983 to 2018 – that's thirty-five years! During this time, new craters and parts of the volcano will form from the slow-spreading lava.

DAY 2

Discussing how one event (a cause) leads to another (an effect) can be a useful way of discussing the relationship between the two events.

1. **Describe a cause and its effect in the Day 1 passage above.**

   ____

   ____

2. **Combine the cause-and-effect sentences below using an appropriate connective phrase (e.g. as a result, this means that, due to, because of, leads to).**

   a BENEE became popular on TikTok. Her songs are played on the radio.

   ____

   b The unpublished manuscript won an award. It will be published by Hachette.

   ____

   c *The Simpsons* makes millions of dollars. The voice actors are millionaires.

   ____

DAY 3

Edit the informative piece below by correcting the four punctuation errors (hyphens, semicolons). **The previous part of this text is on page 94.**

THE ORIGINS OF THE CHINESE ZODIAC

Though we may never know the origins of the Chinese zodiac for sure, the cultural impact that it has had across the globe is impossible to ignore. Many Chinese people consider the influence of the Chinese zodiac when making major life decisions, for instance, in the year of the Dragon, which is associated with good fortune, there is often a spike in birth rates across China as parents hope for children with good fortunes. Similarly, Chinese investors often consider the zodiac when making financial decisions.

As well known Taiwanese-author ShaoLan Hsueh explains, whether or not you believe in the Chinese zodiac, 'the collective decisions made by 1.3 billion people' cause fluctuations in important areas of life, such as economics and healthcare; and ultimately have enormous impacts across the whole world.

DAY 4

❶ **Match the cause with the most logical effect.**

Cause	Effect
video game addiction	becoming an Olympic sprinter
rain	developing a sleep disorder
reading the dictionary	winning a spelling bee
going to athletics camp	a rainbow appearing in the sky

❷ **Research and describe two possible effects of the cause below.**

Cause: overcrowding in classrooms

Effect 1:

Effect 2:

DAY 5

1. **Edit the informative piece below by correcting the four verb tense errors and the four punctuation errors (hyphens, semicolons).** The previous part of this text is on page 95.

THE RISE OF REALITY TV

The influence of reality TV has only continued to grow in the last decade, while it was once simply a source of entertainment for the masses, it is now a tool to obtain power and celebrity. Socialites such as Paris Hilton and Nicole Richie use reality TV in the early 2000s to help bolster their celebrity status, but it was *Keeping Up with the Kardashians* that showed how powerful reality TV could be. The Kardashian-family will create a business empire worth billions of dollars and were able to extend their influence as far as the White-House, with Kim Kardashian meeting President Trump to discuss justice-system reform.

Trump himself gains attention through his reality TV series *The Apprentice*, and his celebrity status will play a role in him becoming; President of the United States.

2. **Write an informative paragraph on one of the cause-and-effect pairings from Day 4, Question 1.**

Topic: ______________________________

____

____

____

____

____

____

____

____

____

____

DAY 1

Edit the informative piece below by correcting the six plural errors. **The previous part of this text is on page 96.**

THE LARGEST APE THAT EVER LIVED

Although palaeontologists (scientist who study fossil) have managed to discover quite a lot about *Gigantopithecus* just from fossilised tooth and jawbones, there is much we may never know about the mysterious creature.

Still, *Gigantopithecus* has undoubtedly made its mark and lives on in our imaginations. Human have long been fascinated by giant beasts. Huge ape-like creature can be found in mythology and folklore all across the world, including the Himalayan yeti, the North American sasquatch and the yowies found in Indigenous Australian legends. More recently, popular media has begun portraying *Gigantopithecus* character directly, including Gutt from the *Ice Age* franchise and King Louie in Disney's 2016 remake of *The Jungle Book*.

DAY 2

The purpose of comparing two things is to highlight meaningful differences and unexpected similarities.

Complete the table below by listing one similarity and one difference between the subjects in each pair. The first one has been done for you.

Subjects	Similarities	Differences
Editorials vs news articles	*Both discuss issues that interest a general audience.*	*Editorials present someone's opinion, whereas a news article reports facts in an objective manner.*
Mars vs Earth		
Alligator vs crocodile		
Photograph vs autobiography		
Australia vs Brazil		

DAY 3

Edit the informative piece below by combining each pair of underlined sentences.
The previous part of this text is on page 97.

THE ORIGINS OF THE MĀORI LANGUAGE

There are some major differences between the eastern Polynesian languages. Take, for example, the language spoken on Pukapuka, one of the most remote islands in the Cook Islands. Pukapukan is an official language of this island. Most Māori speakers cannot make sense of it.

Another difference is the dialect of Māori that is spoken on Palmerston Island. It is mixed with English in a strong Gloucestershire accent.

DAY 4

Complete the Venn diagram below. Include three features that are unique to classroom learning on the left and three features that are unique to remote learning on the right. In the middle, where the circles overlap, write three similarities between the two.

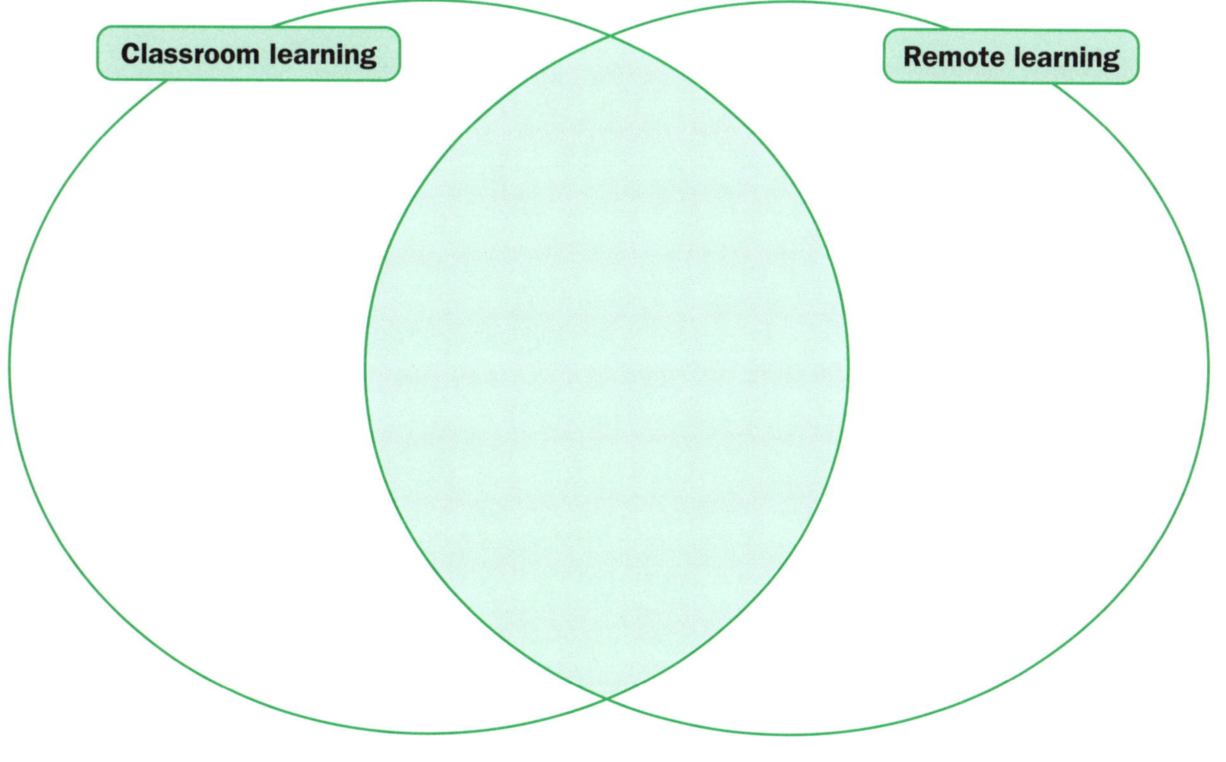

DAY 5

1 **Edit the informative piece below by correcting the two plural errors and combining each pair of underlined sentences.** **The previous part of this text is on page 98.**

THE ROLE OF ARTIFICIAL INTELLIGENCE

The future of AI, the way it will develop and its ongoing role in society are all a mystery. <u>It will have a significant impact on many areas of our day-to-day lives, from transport to healthcare to education. This is certain.</u>

A topics of discussion, however, and frequently the central conflict of a lot of science fiction, is our relationship with it. <u>Will we control AI? Will AI control us?</u> Opinions are divided, even among the expert. Some imagine a future where our lives are effectively run by AI. Others predict that it'll be like many other technological innovations, and may improve or even revolutionise our lives, but it won't replace the human element. Whatever the impact, it's sure to be big.

2 **Write a short informative piece comparing two subjects of your choice. Remember to discuss both similarities and differences between the two.**

Subject 1: ______________________________

Subject 2: ______________________________

____

____

____

____

____

____

____

____

ANALYTICAL WRITING

Daily checklist

WEEK	DAY 1	DAY 2	DAY 3	DAY 4	DAY 5
33	☐	☐	☐	☐	☐
34	☐	☐	☐	☐	☐
35	☐	☐	☐	☐	☐
36	☐	☐	☐	☐	☐
37	☐	☐	☐	☐	☐
38	☐	☐	☐	☐	☐
39	☐	☐	☐	☐	☐
40	☐	☐	☐	☐	☐

DAY 1

Edit the persuasive letter below by correcting the six spelling errors.

CANCEL SCHOOL PHOTO DAYS

Dear Ms Jenkins,

I am writing to request that school photo days be cansellеd. Firstly, the way everyone worries about their appeаrence makes photo day as stressful as exam week! Reknowned psychologist Nella Woods suggests that focusing too much on appearance is harmful to teenagers' mental health.

Secondly, school photos are outdated. Once, they might have been useful to document a special time in one's life. But, Principle, it is 2021! A Deloitte survey showed that 91% of Australians use smartphones to document their lives.

Finally, devoteing a whole day to photos is, frankly, a waste of valuble learning time. A recent Western University study showed that only about 60% of school time is spent learning. I don't think we should lose more to a pointless tradition.

Harriet Jones, Year 8

DAY 2

An argument aims to persuade the audience to agree with one point of view on an issue. The basis of a good argument is a contention supported by reasons.

1. **What is Harriet's main contention in the Day 1 passage above?**

   ____

2. **What reasons does she give for her point of view? Which do you think is the most important reason? Why do you think this?**

   ____

   ____

3. **Do you think the intended audience is likely to be convinced by Harriet's argument? Why or why not?**

   ____

   ____

DAY 3

Edit the analytical piece below by adding four linking words or phrases.

CANCEL SCHOOL PHOTO DAYS: AN ANALYSIS

In her letter, Year 8 student Harriet urges Principal Jenkins to cancel school photo days. She presents three reasons why they should be cancelled. She lists them in order from least to most important.

Harriet's first reason is based on student wellbeing. She argues photo days are 'stressful'. Everyone is worrying about their appearance. She gives a practical reason, stating that school photos are redundant nowadays as most students have smartphones. She concludes with her most important reason – that photo days are 'a waste of valuable learning time' – leaving the reader with a strong final impression.

By presenting three clear, separate reasons based on different concerns, ordered from least to most important, the letter is likely to make Principal Jenkins feel that Harriet's argument is strong and thoughtful.

DAY 4

1. **In the Day 3 passage above, highlight two quotations from the original text.**
2. **Write your own analytical sentence that incorporates a different quote from the Day 1 text.**

   ____

   ____

3. **Circle two instances in the Day 3 passage above that refer to how the reader might respond to Harriet's letter.**
4. **Write your own analytical sentence that refers to how the reader might respond to Harriet's letter.**

   ____

   ____

DAY 5

❶ **Edit the analytical piece below by correcting the two spelling errors and adding two linking words or phrases.**

CANCEL SCHOOL PHOTO DAYS: AN ANALYSIS

Harriet uses evidence from differant sources to support each of the reasons why she believes school photo days should be cancelled. First, she references 'renowned psychologist Nella Woods' as evidence for her claim that school photo days are stressful. This reference to a well-known expert adds authority to Harriet's letter.

Harriet quotes statistics as evidence for her remaining reasons. These indicate that her arguments are based on objective data. They are likely to be reliable. This is reinforced by the fact that her sources are trusted institutions.

This use of evidence in Harriet's letter bolsters her arguement, and positions Principal Jenkins to trust that her views are not just guided by her individual opinion, but are informed by research.

❷ **Complete the analysis of Harriet's letter below.**

Harriet argues that ____

____.

The main reason she gives for her belief is ____

____.

The evidence she gives to support this reason is ____

____.

The principal is likely to feel that Harriet's letter is ____

____.

DAY 1

Edit the persuasive speech below to break up three overly long sentences into shorter ones.

NO MORE BABYSITTING

After yet another exhausting week of enforcing bedtimes, helping with homework and preparing meals for kids *who aren't mine*, I began to wonder – do any of you other first-borns feel taken for granted when it comes to babysitting younger siblings?

I have my own responsibilities to worry about, and I'm sure you do too, so why should we waste our precious time chasing after our little brothers or sisters for nothing in return? You know what they call it when your time is not your own? A job!

Sorry Mum and Dad, but I won't be exploited anymore and, starting from today, I'll be refusing all babysitting duties unless I'm fairly paid for my work.

Rohit

DAY 2

Analysing texts means analysing not just what writers say, but how they say it.

1 Complete the table below to match the word or phrase to the emotion Rohit aims to evoke in his audience.

Word/Phrase	Emotion
exhausting	*sympathy*
waste our precious time	
A job!	

2 Choose the best word or phrase to complete the sentences below.

a In a mostly ______________________ tone, Rohit argues that his parents are treating him unfairly.

b Two words or phrases that help create this tone are ______________________ and ______________________ .

DAY 3

Edit the analytical piece below by varying the beginnings of three sentences that start with 'He'. The first one has been done for you.

NO MORE BABYSITTING: AN ANALYSIS

In his speech, Rohit argues that he shouldn't have to babysit younger siblings for nothing. ~~He begins with~~ *Beginning with* 'After yet another exhausting week' ~~which~~ emphasises that it happens repeatedly and has a negative effect on him. He stresses the work involved by listing his tasks – 'enforcing bedtimes, helping with homework and preparing meals' – and referring to his other 'responsibilities'. He uses an exasperated tone, as shown in expressions such as 'taken for granted' and 'waste our precious time'.

He states that he does these tasks 'for kids *who aren't mine*', indicating that such chores should not be the responsibility of anyone except the child's parents.

DAY 4

Explain the effect on the audience of these sentences from the Day 1 passage. The first one has been done for you.

a 'Do any of you other first-borns feel taken for granted when it comes to babysitting younger siblings?'

The rhetorical question seeks to make the audience feel as exploited as the speaker. This is reinforced by the direct address and the strong language of 'taken for granted'.

b 'I have my own responsibilities to worry about, and I'm sure you do too.'

____

____

c '[W]hy should we waste our precious time chasing after our little brothers or sisters for nothing in return?'

____

____

DAY 5

1 **Edit the analytical piece below by breaking up one overly long sentence into shorter ones and varying the beginnings of two sentences that start with 'Rohit uses'.**

NO MORE BABYSITTING: AN ANALYSIS

Rohit uses emotive language to position the audience to feel sympathy for him for being so overworked and unappreciated, for example, the word 'exploitation' has associations with illegal and immoral behaviour, making it seem that his parents are behaving very unreasonably. Rohit uses the word 'fairly' to create a contrast with how he would like to be treated.

Rohit uses inclusive language, such as 'we', helping his audience to share his frustration and sense of unfairness. Rohit uses a sarcastic tone when he says, 'You know what they call it when your time is not your own? A job!' to position the audience to agree that his current situation is unfair.

2 **Choose three persuasive words or phrases from Rohit's speech. Write one or two analytical sentences about each, identifying why Rohit chose this particular word or phrase (i.e. what effect he was aiming to have on his audience).**

Word/phrase 1: ______________________________

____

____

Word/phrase 2: ______________________________

____

____

Word/phrase 3: ______________________________

____

____

DAY 1

Edit the opinion piece below by correcting the four punctuation errors (ending punctuation, semicolons).

CYCLING ON FOOTPATHS SHOULD BE LEGALISED

Australia, let's face it: we have an abysmal track record when it comes to cycling Last year's National Cycling Participation Survey found that only 14% of the population rode bikes in the previous week. For years cycling rates have been on the decline:

As a die-hard cyclist, I think it's an enormous shame that we are neglecting one of the cheapest; healthiest and most environmentally friendly forms of transport available – but I'm also aware that our busy roads (and irritable drivers) are far from bike friendly. This is why I propose that cycling on footpaths should be legalised right across the country. It's beyond time to make cycling safer for all Australians?

DAY 2

! An opinion piece always aims to persuade the audience to agree with the writer's point of view.

1. **Write a sentence summarising the writer's point of view and their purpose.**

2. **In one or two sentences, summarise the reasons the writer presents for their opinion.**

3. **Highlight words and phrases that the writer uses to try to persuade their audience to agree with their opinion.**

4. **Select one of the words or phrases you identified in Question 3 and write a sentence analysing the intended effect on the reader.**

Daily WRITING & EDITING Practice

DAY 3

Edit the analytical piece below by joining the pairs of underlined sentences.

CYCLING ON FOOTPATHS SHOULD BE LEGALISED: AN ANALYSIS

In this opinion piece on cycling, the writer argues that cycling on footpaths should be legal. This is for health, safety and environmental reasons. They use a firm tone, shown in expressions such as 'let's face it'. It's also shown in the expression 'it's beyond time'. The writer also uses concrete evidence in the form of statistics, which can be seen in the reference to '14% of the population' having ridden bikes in the last week, as well the suggestion that 'cycling rates have been on the decline'. Using figures suggests that the writer is informed about the issue. This adds credibility to their argument. The confident tone, together with the use of statistics, suggests that the writer is making an argument supported by logical reasoning.

DAY 4

1. **Highlight the topic sentence in the Day 3 passage above and explain whether it is supported by the rest of the paragraph.**

   ____

   ____

2. **Complete the sentences below to create topic sentences for further analytical paragraphs like the Day 3 passage above.**

   a The writer aims to make the reader feel that Australia is doing a poor job of managing cycling by ______________________________.

   b They aim to make cycling on footpaths seem sensible by ______________________________

   ______________________________.

   c The writer aims to seem reasonable by ______________________________

   ______________________________.

DAY **5**

❶ **Edit the analytical piece below by correcting the four punctuation errors (ending punctuation, semicolons) and joining the pairs of underlined sentences.**

CYCLING ON FOOTPATHS SHOULD BE LEGALISED: AN ANALYSIS

The writer frequently uses emotive language, for example they refer to the situation as 'abysmal' and an 'enormous shame'. These terms position the reader to feel worried about the situation. They also imply the issue is important and worth caring about. The phrase 'die-hard cyclist' makes the writer seem passionate and knowledgeable. This suggests their opinion is worth listening to.

The writer combines emotive language with inclusive language such as 'our busy roads; and 'we have'. This positions the reader to feel that they and the writer are on the same side, and so they should share the writer's concerns: When used together with the emotive language, this suggests to the reader that if they agree with the writer they will be on the right side of the issue,

❷ **Use one of the topic sentences you created on Day 4, Question 2 to write a new analytical paragraph on 'Cycling on footpaths should be legalised'.**

DAY 1

Edit the advertisement below by correcting the five verb tense errors.

SUNLITE

SunLite has been the zero-waste sun lamp you've were waiting for! Unlike regular solar-powered lamps, SunLite storing light directly from the sun. No more nasty, artificial electricity – SunLite radiating genuine sunshine only.

Lighted up your home the natural way with SunLite!

DAY 2

❗ Visual texts can be interpreted and analysed just like written texts.

1. **What are the main reasons presented for purchasing a SunLite?**

____

____

2. **How do the visual elements support the text?**

____

____

3. **Complete the table below linking the visual elements to the benefits of the product.**

Visual element	Benefit of SunLite
plants	
	cost-effective
sunshine	

DAY 3

Edit the analytical piece below by correcting the four punctuation errors (hyphens, semicolons).

SUNLITE ADVERTISEMENT: AN ANALYSIS

This advertisement uses both written text and an image to present the new solar-powered product 'SunLite' as environmentally friendly, unique and affordable.

The text describes the lamp as 'natural' and 'zero-waste', indicating that SunLite is environmentally friendly. This is reinforced by the image's depiction of a light bulb in a forest environment; emphasising the link to nature. The advertisers also aim to portray SunLite as unique. The phrase 'Unlike regular solar powered lamps' highlights that SunLite is different from competitor products because it uses 'genuine sunshine only'. Finally, the placement of a small pile of coins next to the light bulb indicates that the product is cost effective, this appeals to the audience's desire for value for money.

DAY 4

1. **Identify three main colours you think would be used in the full-colour version of the image in the Day 1 text and list their associations. The first one has been done for you.**

   a *yellow* : *sunlight* , *happiness* , *good weather*

   b ______ : ______ , ______ , ______

   c ______ : ______ , ______ , ______

2. **Underline the parts of the Day 3 passage above that analyse the image.**

3. **Write your own sentence that analyses the intended effect of the image on the audience.**

   ____

   ____

DAY 5

1 **Edit the analytical piece below by correcting the three verb tense errors and the three punctuation errors (hyphens, semicolons).**

SUNLITE ADVERTISEMENT: AN ANALYSIS

The advertisers make use of visual elements to further emphasised SunLite's connection to nature. In the image, the light bulb is placed to the left of two seedlings, as though it has sprouted from the soil. The use of lighting also highlights this connection, the bright-sunlight in the background mirrored the glow with-in the light bulb, visually demonstrating SunLite's solar-powered functioning.

These visual elements work in conjunction with the advertisement's language choices. Words with positive connotations such as 'genuine' and 'natural' are positioned in opposition to descriptors such as 'nasty' and 'artificial'. Through this contrast between 'natural' and 'artificial', the advertisers aim to presented SunLite as the best, most authentic choice in the market for solar-powered lights.

2 **Complete the short analysis of the advertisement.**

The purpose of the ad is to ______________________________ .

Use of language such as ______________________ and ______________________

aims to evoke ______________________ [emotion/s] in the reader. This is reinforced

by the image, which shows ______________________________ [description].

One persuasive feature of the image is ______________________________ .

This is persuasive because ______________________________

______________________________ [effect on the audience].

The image and the written text work together to position the viewer to believe that

SunLite is ______________________________ .

DAY 1

Edit the analytical piece below by correcting the seven plural errors.

FAIRYTALES: AN ANALYSIS

'Fairytales depict stereotypical ideas about women.' Do you agree?

The portrayal of female character in fairytales has evolved over many century. Classic fairytale such as *Cinderella* (1697) and *Snow White* (1812) depict their heroines as weak, passive characters. Cinderella only finds happiness by marrying Prince Charming, while Snow White needs a prince to save her. These scenario support an outdated idea that woman are not strong enough on their own. However, in more modern fairytale adaptation, female characters are drawn as strong and independent. For example, sister Elsa and Anna from the Disney film *Frozen* (2014) are portrayed as complex characters who thrive without romantic interests. So, while classic fairytales depict women as weak and dependent on men, more modern versions focus on their strengths.

DAY 2

When presented with an analytical topic, it is important to understand exactly what the question is asking before developing an answer (i.e. a contention).

Underline the key words in the topics below and rewrite the topic in your own words, using synonyms for the key words. The first one has been done for you.

a '*The Little Mermaid* highlights the importance of having a voice.' Discuss.

'Being able to speak and communicate is a very important message in The Little Mermaid.' Discuss.

b '*Snow White* demonstrates the dangerous consequences of jealousy.' Discuss.

____

c In *Jack and the Beanstalk*, is Jack's decision to climb the beanstalk selfish?

____

Daily WRITING & EDITING Practice

DAY 3

Edit the analytical piece below by correcting the six capitalisation errors.

HARRY POTTER ANALYSIS

'The characters in _Harry Potter_ are used to represent good and evil.' Discuss.

JK rowling's *Harry Potter and the philosopher's Stone* is about the struggle between good and evil. The characters in the book are used to show these two opposing sides. The good side is represented by Harry and his friends. Their goodness is shown by their strong friendship, their kindness to others and their fight against the forces of darkness. Evil is represented by Voldemort, Draco and the dursleys. They are depicted as evil through the way they spread hatred, greed and fear. Voldemort is the most purely evil, with no positive qualities. he acts only to fulfil his own selfish needs and spreads terror throughout the wizarding community. His battle with Harry is depicted as the Ultimate Battle between good and evil in the novel.

DAY 4

In your own words, write a short summary of what each topic below is asking and how you might respond. The first one has been done for you.

a 'Hermione is the real hero of *Harry Potter and the Philosopher's Stone*.' Do you agree?

The topic is asking whether Hermione, rather than Harry, is the hero. I disagree. Although Hermione definitely helps Harry, it is Harry himself who has to fight against Voldemort.

b 'Living with the Dursleys gave Harry strength of character.' Do you agree?

____

____

c 'The teachers at Hogwarts don't protect their students enough from the dangers of the school.' Do you agree?

____

____

Daily WRITING & EDITING Practice

DAY **5**

❶ **Edit the analytical piece below by correcting the four plural errors and the four capitalisation errors.**

STRANGER THINGS ANALYSIS

'Stranger Things **highlights the power of friendship.' Discuss.**

friendship plays a major roles in the Duffer Brothers' 2016 television series *Stranger things*. The event in the first season show how friendship helps the characters to overcome obstacles and gives them a sense of belonging. When will goes missing, his friends Mike, Dustin and Lucas do everything in their power to find him. It is only through teamwork that they are able to defeat the supernatural Beast guarding their friend and rescue him. The character of Eleven, on the other hand, has lived her whole life in a laboratories and has never experienced friendship. The friendships that she develops with Mike, Dustin and Lucas make her feel less lonely and give her life new purposes.

❷ **Write a contention in response to the topics below. The first one has been done for you.**

a '*From the Ashes* (pp. 30, 36, 42, 48) shows that the greatest power in this world is the tears of a phoenix.' Do you agree?

While the tears of a phoenix are magical and able to heal people, From the Ashes suggests that Ioke's love for her brother is stronger.

b '*Summer* (pp. 29, 35, 41, 47) highlights how appearances can be deceiving.' Do you agree?

______

______

c '*All Aboard* (pp. 32, 38, 44, 50) suggests that age is no barrier to being a hero.' Do you agree?

______

______

Daily **WRITING & EDITING** Practice

DAY 1

Edit the analytical piece below by correcting the five spelling errors. The previous part of this text is on page 119.

FAIRYTALES: AN ANALYSIS

Cinderella and Snow White are shown to be passive characters. Cinderella is opressed by her stepmother and stepsisters, forced to do all the housework. But instead of seeking to escape, all she wants is to go to a ball. Significantly, she is saved not by anything that she does, but by her beuty, which leads to her marrying Prince Charming. This is similer to Snow White, who needs male characters to save her from the Evil Queen. The huntsman chooses not to kill her, the seven dwarfes take her in and the prince saves her from a death-like sleep with a kiss. In both stories, it is the brave and hansome prince who saves the day, rather than the female characters the stories are named after.

DAY 2

It is important to plan the structure of an analytical essay before beginning to write it.

Complete the analytical essay plan below for one of your favourite books. (Use the topics from Week 37 as a guide when creating your own.)

TEXT:

TOPIC:

CONTENTION:

REASON 1 SUPPORTING THE CONTENTION:

REASON 2 SUPPORTING THE CONTENTION:

DAY 3

Edit the analytical piece below by correcting the three run-on sentences. **The previous part of this text is on page 120.**

HARRY POTTER ANALYSIS

The kindness and love shown by Harry and his friends demonstrate their goodness, this includes the way they treat each other. Ron (encouraged by his mother) sits beside Harry on the Hogwarts Express because he doesn't know anyone else, Harry, meanwhile, buys all the treats from the cart to share with Ron when he realises he doesn't have any money. Harry shows this same compassion to Professor Quirrell, whom Harry believes is being threatened by Professor Snape: 'Whenever Harry passed Quirrell these days he gave him an encouraging sort of smile.' Unknowingly, Harry is being nice to someone who is secretly evil, he can't help it though; being good is in his nature. He doesn't ever even consider the idea of committing bad deeds, saying, 'I'm never going over to the Dark Side!'

DAY 4

Provide two reasons that support the contentions you listed in Week 37, Day 5. The first one has been done for you.

a 1. *A phoenix's tears can only heal physical ailments, not bring happiness like love can.*

2. *The love of his sister gives Kaleo the strength to climb a mountain, despite his blindness.*

b 1. ______________________

2. ______________________

c 1. ______________________

2. ______________________

Daily **WRITING & EDITING** Practice

DAY 5

❶ **Edit the analytical piece below by correcting the two spelling errors and the two run-on sentences.** **The previous part of this text is on page 121.**

STRANGER THINGS ANALYSIS

The characters in *Stranger Things* are confronted with seemingly inpossible challenges, but their strong bonds as friends help them to succeed, one of the opening scenes of the series, showing Mike, Dustin, Lucas and Will engaged in an intense game of Dungeons & Dragons, highlights the joy of friendship. But when Will goes missing, the power of friendship is put to the test. Mike, Dustin and Lucas never give up hope of finding their friend, when they find Will in a dangerous alternat dimension called the Upside Down, they discover a beastly Demogorgon blocks their path. Together, and with the help of their new friend Eleven, they manage to defeat the beast and rescue Will.

❷ **Using the text and topic from your plan in Day 2, fill in the gaps to create an introduction outline.**

The topic is asking ____

____.

I agree/disagree with the statement in the topic because ____________________

____.

One reason I agree/disagree with the statement in the topic is ____________________

____.

Another reason I agree/disagree with the statement in the topic is ____________________

____.

DAY 1

Edit the analytical piece below by correcting the five subject–verb agreement errors. **The previous part of this text is on page 122.**

FAIRYTALES: AN ANALYSIS

The Disney film *Frozen* portray female characters who are very different from Cinderella and Snow White. It is a tale of two sisters (one of whom turns everything she touches into ice) and explore the idea of female power. Elsa and Anna are both strong, independent women who do not obsess over finding a man. Elsa is concerned with being a good queen and learning to control her powers while Anna only want to help her sister. In contrast to the romantic love at the centre of classic fairytales, *Frozen* focus on sisterly love. Anna sacrifices herself to save Elsa, an act that release their kingdom from an eternal winter. It is their bond as sisters that saves the day.

DAY 2

! The reasons in support of a contention about a text should be backed up by evidence. Evidence usually takes the form of quotes or examples from the text.

1. **Underline the topic sentence in the Day 1 passage above and explain how this passage responds to the topic.**

____

____

2. **Provide a quote from the text that supports one of the reasons you listed in Week 38, Day 4 and explain how it supports the reason. The first one has been done for you.**

Text and reason	Quote and explanation
From the Ashes – The love of his sister gives Kaleo the strength to climb a mountain, despite his blindness.	*'I can't believe we made it.' This quote from Kaleo shows that he never thought he would be able to climb the mountain, and that he was able to do so because of Ioke.*
Summer –	
All Aboard –	

DAY 3

Edit the analytical piece below by correcting the five quotation mark errors. **The previous part of this text is on page 123.**

HARRY POTTER ANALYSIS

'The villains in the novel are identified by the way they treat others. The Dursleys are extremely mean to Harry, giving him no love or affection. They lock him in a cupboard under the stairs, let Dudley bully him and leave him all alone at a busy railway station. The bad characters that Harry encounters at Hogwarts are even worse. Draco Malfoy is a snobby Slytherin boy who threatens Harry on the Hogwarts Express and jinxes Neville without provocation. He is also cruel in the way he speaks to others, telling Neville, If brains were gold, you'd be poorer than Weasley,' and that's saying something.' 'As bad as Malfoy is, he doesn't compare to Voldemort, who is so evil that he murders innocent people for power.'

DAY 4

❶ **Underline a quote in the Day 3 passage above and explain how it supports the argument being made.**

____

____

❷ **Underline another piece of evidence (such as a plot point or information about a character) in the Day 3 passage above and explain how it supports the argument being made.**

____

____

❸ **Suggest another piece of evidence from the books that could have been used to support the argument.**

____

____

DAY **5**

❶ **Edit the analytical piece below by correcting the four subject–verb agreement errors and the four quotation mark errors.** **The previous part of this text is on page 124.**

STRANGER THINGS ANALYSIS

Through the character of Eleven, *Stranger Things* show how friendship can create meaning in our lives. The idea of friendship is foreign to Eleven until she meets Mike, Dustin and Lucas and is accepted into their friendship circle. When she admit to opening the gate to the Upside Down, instead of rejecting her, Mike reassure her, saying you're not the monster … you saved me. He, Dustin and Eleven embrace as the camera pans out on the three of them huddled together, highlighting their close bonds. 'The joy of friendship give Eleven a new purpose in life: to use her powers to protect those she cares about.' At the end of the season, she sacrifices herself to destroy the Demogorgon and save her friends.

❷ **Using one of the reasons listed in your plan from Week 38, write a body paragraph that responds to the topic. Begin with a topic sentence and include at least two pieces of evidence to support your argument.**

DAY 1

Edit the analytical piece below by correcting the five punctuation errors (commas, apostrophes). **The previous part of this text is on page 125.**

FAIRYTALES: AN ANALYSIS

Fairytale's have evolved over time to present more accurate representations of women. Classic fairytales such as *Cinderella* and *Snow White*, showed female character's whose main positive attribute was their beauty. Their personalities were not explored in any meaningful way, and they were shown to be powerless, without their princes. As time has passed, fairytales have started to show female characters who are braver and more intelligent, and who can achieve things without help from a man. This is highlighted in the characters of Elsa and Anna from *Frozen*. These sisters have distinctive attributes and find support in each other and their friends. They represent strong and complex women countering stereotypical ideas seen in classic fairytales.

DAY 2

The purpose of a conclusion to an analytical essay is to remind readers of the strengths of the main argument. It should not introduce new ideas.

Which conclusion do you think is stronger: the Day 1 passage above or the option below? Explain your choice.

All fairytales depict women in a negative light. There's obviously Cinderella and Snow White, but also Ariel from *The Little Mermaid*. She is depicted as a weak character who is willing to give up her voice and her life for a man she met briefly. I don't think she accurately reflects women today. Therefore, my response to the question is yes, I agree: fairytales depict stereotypical ideas about women. But let's not forget about how the male characters are depicted. They aren't given much personality either. They only exist in these stories to save damsels in distress and marry them.

Explanation: ______________________________

____

____

____

DAY 3

Edit the analytical piece below by combining each pair of underlined sentences.
The previous part of this text is on page 126.

HARRY POTTER ANALYSIS

Harry Potter and the Philosopher's Stone uses characters to highlight the differences between good and evil. The good characters are marked by their caring actions. Harry and his friends in Gryffindor extend kindness to everyone they encounter, even those who don't deserve it. <u>There is a contrast. The evil characters are marked by their cruel actions.</u> They take pleasure in hurting other people and seeing them suffer. Characters on each side cannot understand those on the other side. <u>Harry uses all his strength to avoid becoming evil. Voldemort 'didn't realise that love ... leaves its own mark'.</u>

DAY 4

1. **Highlight a sentence in the Day 3 passage above that restates the main argument.**
2. **How does the conclusion above differ from the introduction to this essay (p.120)?**

___

___

___

3. **Expand on the conclusion above by adding a statement that reinforces the earlier arguments made.**

___

___

___

DAY 5

❶ **Edit the analytical piece below by correcting the two punctuation errors (commas, apostrophes) and combining each pair of underlined sentences.** **The previous part of this text is on page 127.**

STRANGER THINGS ANALYSIS

The characters in *Stranger Things* show how powerful friendship can be. The close bonds of friendship are what drive Mike, Dustin and Lucas to look for Will. The adults around them give up hope. Their willingness to accept Eleven into their group also help's them along their journey. Working together, they are able to overcome the threat of the Demogorgon. They save their friend from the Upside Down. In the process of helping the others save Will Eleven discovers a new reason for being. She now understands the importance of human connection and has found happiness in friendship.

❷ **Write a conclusion to the essay topic you listed in your plan in Week 38, Day 2.**